CHEMICAL WAREHOUSING
the storage of packaged dangerous substances

D1744281

HSG71

HSE BOOKS

First published 1992 as Storage of packaged dangerous substances
Second edition 1998

ISBN 0 7176 1484 0

This guidance is issued by the Health and Safety Executive. Following the guidance
is not compulsory and you are free to take other action. But if you do follow the
guidance you will normally be doing enough to comply with the law. Health and
safety inspectors seek to secure compliance with the law and may refer to this
guidance as illustrating good practice.

CONTENTS

PREFACE

This book provides information on the hazards associated with the storage of packaged dangerous substances. It sets out practical measures on the design, construction, operation and maintenance of storage areas and buildings used for storing packaged dangerous substances. These measures are designed to protect people at work and others who may be affected by the storage of packaged dangerous substances.

The guidance is aimed at those directly responsible for the safe storage of packaged dangerous substances in all general work activities.

Safety specialists and trade organisations or associations may wish to use this publication as a basis for more specific guidance for their own members.

While the references to British or other standards made in this book specify their year of issue, it is recognised that they are regularly updated and many are harmonised into a common European Standard. Invariably, any such replacement standards may be used in place of the standards quoted.

2003 reprint

The text of this book has not been updated at reprint, as the technical advice it contains remains sound. The law has, however, changed since 1998.

Health and safety law relating to flammable materials has been completely revised. Readers are advised to refer to *Dangerous substances and explosive atmospheres. Dangerous Substances and Explosive Atmospheres Regulations 2002. Approved code of practice and guidance* L138 published by HSE Books in 2003, ISBN 0 7176 2203 7.

Fire safety law has also been amended by the Fire Precautions (Workplace)(Amendment) Regulations 1999 SI 1999/1877. Readers are advised to refer to *Fire Safety - An employer's guide* published by the Stationery Office, ISBN 0 11 34122 9.

OBJECTIVES

The objectives of this publication are to:

(a) help in the assessment and reduction of the risks associated with the storage of packaged dangerous substances;

(b) increase the awareness of the potential hazards associated with the storage of packaged dangerous substances;

(c) advise on safe management procedures and precautions to reduce injuries and damage caused by incidents involving the storage of packaged dangerous substances. Ill health is also important, but it is not addressed in any detail in this book;

(d) give guidance on the appropriate standards for the design and construction of storage areas and buildings used for storing packaged dangerous substances at ambient temperature and pressure;

(e) advise on the need for appropriate precautions, maintenance, training and good housekeeping where packaged dangerous substances are stored.

INTRODUCTION

General

1   This book provides you with guidance on the control measures you could adopt for the safe storage of packaged dangerous substances. It replaces an earlier publication HSG71 *The storage of packaged dangerous substances*. It sets out the steps you can take to control the risk of incidents involving dangerous substances. The incidents causing the greatest concern have generally resulted from the outbreak of fire.

2   The guidance applies to all storage locations whether in the open air, or in specifically designed buildings. It applies to new and existing sites where reasonably practicable.

Legal requirements

3   This guidance will help you in your assessment of the risks arising from the storage of packaged dangerous substances, and it gives advice on how you can control the risks.

4   Assessment, by employers and the self-employed, of the risks to employees and others who may be affected by the work activities is one of the requirements of the Management of Health and Safety at Work Regulations 1992.[1]

5   This book also advises on how to comply with the relevant parts of the Health and Safety at Work etc Act 1974,[2] at places where packaged dangerous substances are stored, and with other relevant legislation (see Appendix 1).

6   Current legislation, guidance literature and standards are referred to in the text, and are detailed in Appendix 1 and References and further reading. They are subject to amendment from time to time. You need to ensure that the requirements, at the time any work or alterations are carried out, reflect the current legal requirements and good accepted practice.

7   The glossary at the back of this book explains the particular terms used in this guidance.

What is risk assessment?

8   A risk assessment is an organised look at your work activities using the following five steps:

Step 1:   Look for the hazards.

Step 2:   Decide who may be harmed and how.

Step 3:   Evaluate the risks arising from the hazards and decide whether existing precautions are adequate or if more should be done.

Step 4:   Record your significant findings.

Step 5:   Review your assessment from time to time and revise it if necessary.

Advice on carrying out risk assessments is contained in an HSE leaflet.[3]

9   The remaining sections of this book will help you to identify many of the hazards associated with the storage of packaged dangerous substances, and give guidance on how to reduce the risks.

10   The guidance will show many of the issues you need to consider when carrying out your risk assessments. It will help in deciding which precautions are needed concerning the storage arrangements for dangerous substances. A complete risk assessment will also have to consider other hazards, for example manual handling, trips and slips, and transport safety, which are not within the scope of this book.

Scope

Definition of 'dangerous substance'

11   This book covers substances or preparations which are dangerous as defined by:

(a)   the Carriage of Dangerous Goods (Classification, Packaging and Labelling) and Use of Transportable Pressure Receptacles Regulations 1996;[4]

(b)   the Chemicals (Hazard Information and Packaging for Supply) Regulations 1994 (as amended);[5] and

(c)   the Highly Flammable Liquids and Liquefied Petroleum Gases Regulations 1972;[6]

when they are contained in packages such as drums, gas cylinders, bottles, boxes, intermediate bulk containers (IBCs), and sacks.

12   Manufacturers, importers and other suppliers have responsibilities under this legislation for the classification and labelling of dangerous substances and preparations. The purpose of the classification is to identify the properties of substances and preparations that may constitute a hazard during normal handling and use.

13   It is important to note that there is a difference between hazard (the inherent properties of a chemical) and risk (the probability of the hazardous properties of the chemical causing harm to people or the environment). Classification concerns identification of the hazard not the risk.

Applying the standards

14   This guidance gives advice to operators of storage sites for packaged dangerous substances, and applies to transit or distribution warehouses, open-air storage compounds and facilities associated with a chemical production site or end-user.

15   The advice in this book provides you with suitable standards for the design and location of storage facilities for packaged dangerous substances.

16   It may be inappropriate or impractical for you to adopt all the recommendations in this book, particularly at existing premises. However the law requires you to make any improvements which are reasonably practicable, taking into account the risks at the premises and the cost and feasibility of additional precautions.

17   This book describes a number of ways of achieving an adequate standard of safety. Further advice on how to use it at specific sites can be obtained from whoever inspects the site for health and safety, usually HSE or the local authority.

Environmental protection

18   Many substances, which may not be particularly harmful to humans, are eco-toxic. Spillages or emissions of dangerous substances can cause environmental harm and may have consequences in criminal law and/or civil law. Such emissions may be subject to controls under the Environmental Protection Act 1990,[7] and if water pollution occurs, under the Water Resources Act 1991[8] in England and Wales or the Control of Pollution Act 1974[9] (as amended) in Scotland.

19   Although this guidance does not attempt to cover environmental issues in any detail, the advice it contains for safe storage conditions will help provide some protection for the environment.

20   Further guidance is available from the Environment Agency (or in Scotland, the Scottish Environment Protection Agency (SEPA)) or from local authorities, all of which enforce the Environmental Protection Act.[7]

Additional advice and information

21   You can find more appropriate advice, in documents listed in the Further reading section, on the following topics:

(a)   the storage and carriage of highly flammable liquids;

(b)   the storage of transportable gas cylinders;

(c)   the storage of agrochemicals;

(d)   the storage of explosives;

(e)   the storage of radioactive substances;

(f)   the storage of infectious substances; and

(g)   specific industries.

22   The advice in this book does not apply to:

(a)   fixed storage vessels;

(b)   bulk carriage by road or rail;

(c)   tank containers with a capacity greater than 3 cubic metres; or

(d)   freight containers, or packaged dangerous substances in freight containers during transport.

Dangerous substances which are pesticides

23   All pesticides are subject to Part III of the Food and Environment Protection Act 1985[10] (FEPA), and they must be approved either:

(a)   under the Control of Pesticides Regulations 1986[11] (as amended); or

(b)   under the Plant Protection Products Regulations 1995[12] (as amended) and the Plant Protection Products (Basic Conditions) Regulations 1997.[13]

24   The FEPA Part III Code of Practice[14] and HSE Agricultural Information Sheet No 16[15] are available for guidance on the safe storage of pesticides.

25   However, you may use this book to gain more information on how to deal with the specific hazards of such pesticides.

HAZARDS

Introduction

26   The storage of packaged dangerous substances may create serious risks, not only to people working at the storage site, but also to the emergency services, the general public off-site and the environment.

27   The incidents causing the greatest concern have generally resulted from the outbreak of fire. Such fires expose employees, members of the emergency services and the general public to the threat of radiated heat, missiles, harmful smoke and fumes. In addition, a major fire may cause the widespread distribution of substances harmful to the environment, either in the smoke plume or in the water used to fight the fire.

28   Common causes of such incidents include:

(a)   lack of awareness of the properties of the dangerous substances;

(b)   operator error, due to lack of training;

(c)   inappropriate storage conditions with respect to the hazards of the substances;

(d)   inadequate design, installation or maintenance of buildings and equipment;

(e)   exposure to heat from a nearby fire;

(f)   poor control over sources of ignition, including smoking and smoking materials;

(g)   vandalism and arson.

Hazard classification

29   In any situation, the precautions needed to achieve a reasonable standard of control will vary but must take into account the properties of the substance to be stored. Different substances create very different risks because of their hazards. It is therefore important that the standards adopted at a particular site are based on an understanding of the physical and chemical properties of the substances concerned. Interactions between different substances, especially those which are incompatible, may create additional hazards.

30   Other important factors are the overall quantities of the substances to be stored and the maximum size of individual packages. Obviously the risk from a packaged dangerous substance is dependent on the amount of dangerous substance present within any given package. The type of packaging used can also influence the fire hazard.

31   Many dangerous substances are harmful to health if they are inhaled, ingested or come into contact with skin or eyes. You can obtain information on the health hazards of a particular substance, and on any specific precautions required, from the material safety data sheet (MSDS) or from the supplier. The Control of Substances Hazardous to Health Regulations 1994[16] require employers to assess the risks from exposure to hazardous substances and put in place any precautions needed. Paragraphs 38-42 give further details on health precautions.

32   The hazards of any particular substance should have been classified according to a recognised classification system. Many substances arriving on site will be marked with carriage labelling. This guidance refers to the system used in the Carriage of Dangerous Substances (Classification, Packaging and Labelling) and Use of Transportable Pressure Receptacles Regulations 1996.[4] Goods in international transit may be marked using the similar ADR[17] scheme. For those companies which do not have transport operations, the dangerous goods will be classified by the Chemicals (Hazard Information and Packaging for Supply) Regulations.[5] In some cases the classification of a material differs depending on the regulatory requirements. For example, the supply Regulations classify liquids as flammable if the flashpoint is less than or equal to 55°C, while the transport Regulations classify liquids as flammable if the flashpoint is less than or equal to 61°C.

33   The various classification categories are given in the following paragraphs. Note that Class 1 (explosives), Class 6.2 (infectious substances) and Class 7 (radioactive substances) are not considered in this book. Guidance on these goods is given elsewhere.[18,19]

34   Remember that other more unusual hazards may be encountered from stored chemicals, for example:

(a)   solids which melt, flow and then block drainage systems;

(b)   materials which generate heat if water is added;

(c)   materials which significantly assist the development of a fire even if air is excluded.

Class 2 - Gases, compressed, liquefied, or dissolved under pressure.

In addition to the labelling required under the various regulations,[4,5,6] cylinders are often colour coded to provide indication of their contents. A new European standard BS EN 1089-3,[20] relating to the colour coding of transportable gas cylinders, replaces BS 349, which has been withdrawn.

Minor leaks from cylinders of compressed gases may disperse more readily if the cylinders are stored in the open air. Cylinders of liquefied gases should be stored in an upright position so that any leaks from valves etc will be of vapour or gas rather than liquid.

Most types of cylinder will explode if exposed to intense heat, causing a risk of impact to people in the vicinity even if the cylinder contents are non-hazardous. Acetylene cylinders in particular are liable to explode without warning, during or for some time after exposure to heat, because of the self-decomposition of the product.

Where flammable or toxic gas cylinders are stored in buildings, good ventilation is needed to ensure that minor leaks will disperse safely. When considering storage locations and determining ventilation design criteria, your assessment will need to consider the densities of the gases involved, for example whether they are heavier or lighter than air.

Class 3 - flammable liquids

Under the Carriage of Dangerous Substances (Classification, Packaging and Labelling) and Use of Transportable Pressure Receptacles Regulations 1996,[4] liquids are classified as flammable if they have a flashpoint below 61°C.

This definition of flammable liquid includes all liquids classified as flammable, highly flammable and extremely flammable for supply according to the Chemicals (Hazard Information and Packaging for Supply) Regulations,[5] and those defined as highly flammable in the Highly Flammable Liquids and Liquefied Petroleum Gases Regulations 1972.[6]

Flammable liquid fires can grow rapidly once the integrity of the container is breached, the fire spreading quickly as the escaping liquid flows from the stored material. If the fire comes into contact with other flammable or oxidising materials, it will increase significantly in size, and there will be more difficulty bringing it under control. Sealed containers may explode if exposed to intense heat. Depending on ground conditions at the time, liquids may travel some distance while a leak remains undetected.

Precautions to be taken include storing flammable liquids in a cool dry place, away from sources of ignition and heat, and in securely closed containers specifically designed for the purpose. It is preferable for the store to be in the open air, but in all cases adequate ventilation at high and low level will be needed to disperse any vapours from leaking containers.

Class 4

This class contains materials with a variety of hazards and physical properties. Some are low melting point solids, or solids which are kept under a protective layer of inert liquid or gas. The types of substance included are described briefly in the following paragraphs, under the three recognised divisions of the class.

You should obtain advice on each particular type of substance from the supplier. This needs to include information of any special conditions required for safe storage, for example, temperature limitations, sensitivity to impact, friction, impurities or water.

4.1 - flammable solids

These are readily combustible solids that can be ignited by brief contact with a source of ignition or be sensitive to friction, and that will continue to burn after removal of the source of ignition. Examples are matches, fire lighters, nitrocellulose and sulphur.

Self-reactive substances are included in this division. These may decompose with the evolution of heat and fumes at moderate temperatures. Examples include various azo compounds.

Also included in this division are desensitised explosives. These contain sufficient water, solvent or plasticiser to suppress their explosive properties. You need to take care that the water or solvent-wetted explosives are not able to dry out. Examples include picric acid and urea nitrate.

4.2 - self-reactive and related substances

Pyrophoric (spontaneously combustible) substances have packaging which is designed to exclude air. If air enters a damaged package the substances may start to burn at room temperature or when gently heated. Examples include yellow phosphorus and some metal alkyls.

Oxidative self-heating substances may react with the air, and so raise the temperature to the point at which spontaneous combustion takes place. This is normally a slow process which can be controlled by restricting the pack size, limiting storage duration, monitoring temperatures or excluding air. Examples include some types of carbon dust and oily natural products.

4.3 - substances dangerous when wet

These substances react with water and evolve flammable gases. Fire involving, or in the vicinity of, such materials should obviously not be tackled with water. Examples include calcium carbide, metal hydrides, powders of reactive metals such as magnesium or aluminium, and the alkali metals such as sodium.

Class 5 - oxidising substances and organic peroxides

These are substances which, although not generally in themselves combustible, can assist other materials to burn rapidly even if air is excluded. When heated in a fire, many of these substances decompose and give off oxygen which can cause an increase in the rate of burning with possible catastrophic consequences.

There have been a small number of incidents where relatively large packaged quantities of these materials, such as sodium chlorate, have been involved in violent explosions when engulfed in fire. Guidance on the maximum stack size for ammonium nitrate is provided in an HSE publication[21] (equivalent guidance for sodium chlorate will be available from HSE later in 1998).

5.1 - oxidising substances

Most oxidising substances are extremely reactive. They may be solids or liquids. They need to be stored away from flammable materials, so preventing any contamination or any possibility of them becoming involved in a fire. They may be stored with other similar strong oxidising agents provided they are compatible.

5.2 - organic peroxides

Organic peroxides are a particularly reactive type of oxidising substance. They may be solids, liquids or pastes, and have one or more of the following properties:

(a) be liable to explosive decomposition;

(b) burn rapidly;

(c) be sensitive to impact or friction;

(d) react dangerously with other substances;

(e) decompose at comparatively low temperatures.

Some organic peroxides may need to be marked with a subsidiary explosion risk label. Organic peroxides need to be stored separately from flammable, corrosive and toxic materials. Advice on the storage and handling of organic peroxides is given in the HSE guidance note CS21.[22] Specific advice and information on particular organic peroxides can be obtained from the material safety data sheets (MSDS) or the supplier.

Class 6 - toxic substances

The main risk from toxic substances during storage is failure of containment. Appropriate pre-planning can minimise the consequences of isolated punctured drums or burst packages.

However in the event of fire, such protection is likely to be compromised by the failure of many containers due to the effects of flame and heat. As well as posing an immediate threat to anybody in the vicinity, for example fire fighters, the toxic substance can also be spread large distances in the plume of smoke, or they may be washed into water courses by fire-fighting operations.

The precautions necessary to minimise these risks depend on the quantities of toxic substances involved, their degree of toxicity, and their persistence in the environment.

Toxic substances vary widely in the hazard they create. During storage, the acute hazards arising from short-term exposure, due to for example drum failure, are more likely to arise than the chronic effects from low-level long-term exposure. In particular, any labelling under the Carriage of Dangerous Substances (Classification, Packaging and Labelling) and Use of Transportable Pressure Receptacles Regulations 1996[4] will give basic advice on the primary hazards and precautions, but material safety data sheets (MSDS) will need to be consulted for fuller information.

Class 8 - corrosive substances

Dangerous substances may be classified as corrosive because they burn the skin or otherwise harm anyone coming into contact with them. Many corrosive substances will also react with incompatible unsuitable packaging or metals, for example storage racking. Leaking corrosive substances may damage the packaging of other dangerous substances, creating further leaks.

Class 9 - miscellaneous dangerous substances

This class includes such diverse substances as asbestos, substances that are dangerous to the environment, and fertiliser formulations conforming to UN specification No 2071. You need to consider the specific characteristics of any material in this class before accepting it for storage.

SAFETY PRECAUTIONS

Introduction

35   This book describes some ways of achieving safe storage. Other ways may be better for particular installations as long as your risk assessment shows that they provide an equivalent or higher overall level of safety.

36   The precautions outlined here are designed to minimise the risks from the storage of packaged dangerous substances, but they may not take into account possible damage from an external source such as an incident at another site.

37   The hazards of particular classes of substances have been discussed in the previous section. An assessment of the likelihood that people will be harmed by the presence of the dangerous substances is needed when considering:

(a)   whether the precautions present at an existing storage site are adequate and suitable; or

(b)   which precautionary measures are to be included in the design of a new installation.

This risk assessment is required by the Management of Health and Safety at Work Regulations 1992.[1] Detailed information in the form of a safety report has to be prepared if regulations 7-12 of the Control of Industrial Major Accident Hazards Regulations 1984 (CIMAH)[23] (as amended) apply at your site.

Health precautions

38   Many precautions for reducing fire and explosion risks will also control the health risks. However some additional measures may be necessary since the concentrations of vapours or dusts capable of damaging human health are usually significantly below flammable levels. The Control of Substances Hazardous to Health Regulations 1994[16] require employers to prevent or control exposure to harmful substances. Guidance on these Regulations is contained in the Approved Codes of Practice (ACOPs) *General COSHH ACOP (Control of Substances Hazardous to Health), and Carcinogens ACOP (Control of Carcinogenic Substances) and*

Biological Agents ACOP (Control of Biological Agents). Control of Substances Hazardous to Health Regulations 1994.[24]

39   You need to adopt a safe system of work when dealing with spillages. A number of control measures are possible, and these are described in the spillage control section of this book. Material safety data sheets (MSDS) will detail any specific action to be taken for dealing with spillages. You need to have these available for all the substances stored on site.

40   Spillages need to be cleaned up promptly and the material disposed of safely. You should provide precautions against skin and eye contact, such as gloves, protective clothing and goggles. Suitable respiratory protection may be needed during clean-up operations. Substances new to the site should not be handled until suitable personal protective equipment is available.

41   When corrosive materials have been spilt, due care needs to be taken to ensure that employees wear clothing with the necessary resistance to the substance during operations to clean up the spillage. This clothing should be removed immediately if contaminated with the dangerous substance. Contaminated clothing should not be sent for cleaning with general laundry, or cleaned at an employee's home. It may be cleaned by specialist laundries, or disposed of as dangerous waste.

42   Spillages of dangerous substances in a fine dusty state should not be cleared up by dry brushing. Vacuum cleaners should be used in preference, and for toxic materials, one conforming to type H of British Standard BS 5415[25] should be used. For combustible dusts the vacuum cleaner should not be capable of acting as a source of ignition (see the section *Electrical equipment,* paragraphs 118-125).

Risk assessment

43   For the majority of warehouses storing dangerous substances there are four main events which individually or jointly have the potential to cause significant harm or damage:

(a)   fire;

(b)   explosion;

(c)   release of a toxic substance;

(d)   release of a corrosive substance.

Your risk assessment needs to consider how these events could occur. Examples include:

Fire: - ignition following a spill or release;

            - self-combustion;

            - arson;

            - electrical faults - heaters, cookers, motors etc;

            - hazardous activities - welding, shrink-wrapping, smoking, battery charging etc;

            - external events - lightning, impact, fire in an adjacent property.

Explosion: - fire;

            - spills of incompatible chemicals or flammable liquids/gases.

Large spills: - containment failure;

            - impact by vehicles or other objects;

            - operator error - filling, discharging etc.

44   The precautions needed not only include building and engineering design and installation standards, but also good management practices and operational procedures. The remainder of this book considers the various precautionary measures that can help to ensure safety in the storage of packaged dangerous goods.

45   You do not have to do anything if the risks are already low enough. However, if there is a significant risk that people may be harmed from an incident, you may have to consider additional measures.

46   If the CIMAH Regulations[23] apply at your site then the risk assessment needs to be very detailed, covering off-site risks to people and the environment. HSE has issued guidance[26] on the Regulations, and in particular on what information should be included in a safety report under regulation 7(1).

47   Essentially you need to identify the pathways to events which could lead to a major accident. These might be the dispersal of toxic chemicals in a smoke plume, or polluted fire water run-off contaminating local water courses. The safeguards in place to minimise the likelihood and the consequences of a major accident will need to be of a high standard. To minimise the risks from a major fire, you will need precautions such as:

(a)   fire-resisting compartmentation;

(b)   means of detecting any outbreak of fire and its subsequent control; and

(c)   means of containing any polluted fire water run-off.

Management control

Risk management

48   At all sites where packaged dangerous substances are to be stored, the site management need to consider the risks created and the means adopted to control such risks. The storage of multi-hazard goods together is a high-risk activity demanding high-level management considerations.

49   It is recommended that individual risk management policies be developed for all warehouses or other premises used to store packaged dangerous substances. The degree of detail in these policies is clearly dependent on various factors, for example:

(a)   quantities stored;

(b)   specific hazards of the materials;

(c)   location of warehouse(s).

50   A senior member of staff should be directly responsible for safe warehousing operations. Safety management needs to be a key responsibility of the position. It is important that this person is responsible for the identification, assessment, handling and storage of all the dangerous goods held on site. Clearly this person (or people) needs to be competent to do the job, and should be adequately trained and have sufficient knowledge.

51   Written operating procedures need to be developed covering matters such as the selection of storage locations, dealing with spillages, and security arrangements etc. Liaison with the enforcing authority and the emergency services may be appropriate. Remember that arrangements will be needed for the control of visitors or contractors.

Information and training

52   Adequate training and knowledge of the properties of dangerous substances are essential for their safe storage. Training is also a requirement of the Management of Health and Safety at Work Regulations 1992.[1] Carrying out risk assessments required by these Regulations will identify how much information, training and retraining are needed. Further guidance on these Regulations is contained in an Approved Code of Practice.[27]

53   All staff on the site need to be informed of the risks of storing packaged dangerous substances, and the precautions necessary to safely store substances which have different hazards. Those responsible for the operation of the store need specific training in emergency procedures. Periodic retraining will normally be required. The training should include the following aspects:

(a)   the types of dangerous goods stored, their properties, incompatibilities and hazards, including hazard label recognition and understanding of the contents of MSDSs;

(b)   general procedures for safe handling;

(c)   use of protective clothing and procedures for dealing with leaks and spillages;

(d)   housekeeping and record keeping;

(e)   reporting of faults and incidents, including minor leaks and spills;

(f)   emergency procedures, including raising the alarm and the use of appropriate fire-fighting equipment.

There should be written procedures for the storage of packaged dangerous substances, and these need to be used as the basis for training.

Maintenance and modifications

54   Many incidents involving fires occur during, or as a result of, maintenance and repairs. The likelihood is increased if the work is done by staff or outside contractors who have little knowledge of the hazards associated with the hazardous goods stored. You need to ensure that any contractors who work on site are competent to carry out the work required.

55   The Health and Safety at Work etc Act 1974[2] and the Management of Health and Safety at Work Regulations 1992[1] place duties, to ensure safe working practices, on both the company using the services and the contractor. Guidance is available on selecting and managing contractors.[28]

56   It is essential that no maintenance work is done until:

(a)   the potential hazards of the work have been clearly identified and assessed;

(b)   the precautions needed have been specified in detail;

(c)   the necessary safety equipment has been provided; and

(d)   adequate and clear instruction has been given to all those concerned.

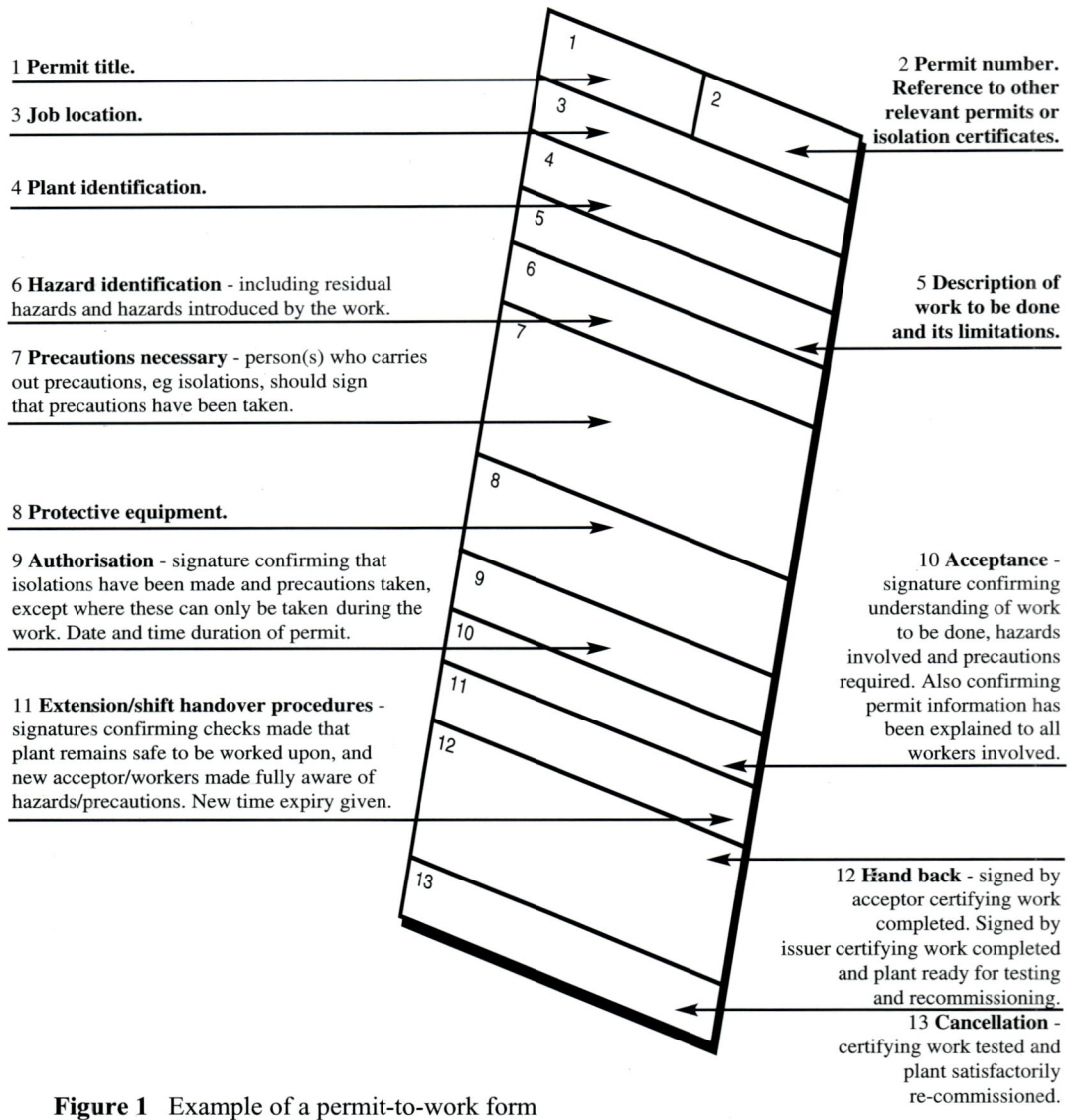

1 **Permit title.**

2 **Permit number.** Reference to other relevant permits or isolation certificates.

3 **Job location.**

4 **Plant identification.**

6 **Hazard identification** - including residual hazards and hazards introduced by the work.

5 **Description of work to be done and its limitations.**

7 **Precautions necessary** - person(s) who carries out precautions, eg isolations, should sign that precautions have been taken.

8 **Protective equipment.**

9 **Authorisation** - signature confirming that isolations have been made and precautions taken, except where these can only be taken during the work. Date and time duration of permit.

10 **Acceptance** - signature confirming understanding of work to be done, hazards involved and precautions required. Also confirming permit information has been explained to all workers involved.

11 **Extension/shift handover procedures** - signatures confirming checks made that plant remains safe to be worked upon, and new acceptor/workers made fully aware of hazards/precautions. New time expiry given.

12 **Hand back** - signed by acceptor certifying work completed. Signed by issuer certifying work completed and plant ready for testing and recommissioning.

13 **Cancellation** - certifying work tested and plant satisfactorily re-commissioned.

Figure 1 Example of a permit-to-work form

57   In most cases, a permit-to-work (PTW) system should be used to control those maintenance operations[29] which create a source of ignition, or could cause damage to the packages. PTWs are formal management documents. They should only be issued by those with clearly assigned authority to do so. The requirements stated in them must be complied with, before the permit is issued and before the work covered by it is undertaken. Individual PTWs should relate to clearly defined individual pieces of work. PTWs should normally include (see also Figure 1):

(a)   the location and nature of the work intended;

(b)   identification of the hazards, including the residual hazards and those introduced by the work itself;

(c)   the precautions necessary, for example, isolations;

(d)   the personal protective equipment required;

(e)   the proposed time and duration of the work;

(f)   the limits of time for which the permit is valid; and

(g)   the person in direct control of the work.

58   Further advice on PTWs is available in an HSE leaflet.[30]

59   There are some simple controls you can adopt to reduce the risks of fire or explosion during maintenance work. You need to make sure that materials, which can burn or be affected by fire, are removed from the work area. If it is not reasonably practicable to remove such materials, then you should position suitable screens or partitions to protect the hazardous inventory. Once the work has finished, you need to thoroughly inspect the area for about an hour to ensure that there is no smouldering material present.

Hazard management

Introduction

60   The properties of a substance, how it is stored and the control of ignition sources are all major factors in determining the likelihood of a fire or explosion incident occurring. Whether a fire will spread and escalate depends on many factors including:

(a)   fire loading, ie the amount of combustible material present;

(b)   fire spread characteristics of the substance;

(c)   storage arrangements;

(d)   effectiveness of fire protection systems;

(e)   building design.

Receipt of goods

61   You need to make sure that the hazards of a consignment containing packaged dangerous substances are identified before being accepted. This can be achieved by discussion or correspondence with the supplier. All suppliers, manufacturers and importers of dangerous substances must comply with the Chemicals (Hazard Information and Packaging for Supply) Regulations.[5] This requirement ensures that:

(a)   the hazard of the substance has been classified;

(b)   the substance is suitably labelled with specific risk and safety phrases, and packaged accordingly; and

(c)   information, in the form of a material safety data sheet, is available.

62   Substances which have been transported need to comply with the Carriage of Dangerous Goods (Classification, Packaging and Labelling) and Use of Transportable Pressure Receptacles Regulations 1996.[4] Goods transported from other EU countries may be labelled using the ADR scheme.[17] This scheme requires packages to be labelled with very similar, or in some cases, identical information to that needed under the Regulations.

63   Essentially, all packaged dangerous goods on arrival at your site should be clearly identifiable and with the necessary information available for you to assess the applicable storage requirements. You will need to check that the contents of each consignment or the individual packages are as detailed on the shipping documentation.

64   Any goods which are not readily identified should not be sent to store. You need procedures for handling such substances, and it is important that your staff are properly trained in, and familiar with, the arrangements. This may mean that you have arrangements for contacting the supplier for help, or for storing the material in an area remote from other materials and premise boundaries. You may have to refuse to accept the material, or request that the supplier removes the material from the site promptly.

Segregation policy

65   Once the consignment has been accepted, your next step in the assessment process is to determine from the hazards of the material where it should be stored. This assessment needs to

be done in advance of the receipt of goods and will determine suitable segregation policies so as to reduce the potential for ignition, and it will also determine the potential severity of a fire.

66   Often it is not a dangerous substance which is the first material ignited in a fire. In many cases it is other combustible materials which act as the initial source. Typical cases can involve plastic packaging, pallets, rubbish ignited by a discarded cigarette or a spark from inappropriately controlled hot work. Similarly, a small quantity of dangerous substances stored within a general goods warehouse could significantly increase the severity of the fire. This then increases the dangers for on-site personnel, the fire brigade and people off-site.

67   The intensity of a fire, or its rate of growth, may be increased if incompatible materials are stored together. For example, oxidising agents will greatly increase the severity of a flammable liquid fire. In addition, a fire may grow and involve dangerous substances which in themselves are not combustible. In this way, toxic materials can be widely dispersed in the smoke plume or carried in the fire-fighting water, leading to potential consequences off-site to people or the environment. The risk of fire can be reduced by separating dangerous substances from packaging materials. This can be achieved by storing dangerous substances in dedicated warehouses or suitable compartments of warehouses, and storing all packaging materials, spare pallets etc in other buildings or compartments.

68   It is the segregation policy which should be used to prevent these types of escalation. If you store a large range of multi-hazard stock, it will not be feasible for each individual substance to be assessed and stored accordingly. Use can be made of the various classification and labelling systems described earlier, as this can greatly simplify the assessment.

69   In cases where a substance is likely to degrade during storage, you need to consult the suppliers concerning the possible hazardous effects of such degradation. Ask them to provide you with:

(a)   the remedial actions to be taken;

(b)   the recommended storage conditions;

(c)   maximum storage times; and

(d)   inspection frequencies.

70   Table 1 gives recommendations for the segregation of dangerous substances according to their hazard classification. The table excludes Class 1 (explosives), Class 6.2 (infectious substances) and Class 7 (radioactive substances). Guidance for the storage of these classes of dangerous goods is contained elsewhere.[18,19]

Table 1
The table shows general recommendations for the separation or segregation of different classes of dangerous substances.

CLASS		CLASS 2 — Flammable gas (2)	CLASS 2 — Compressed gas (2)	CLASS 2 — Toxic gas (2)	CLASS 3 — Flammable liquid (3)
COMPRESSED GASES 2.1 Flammable	2 (Flammable gas)		KEEP APART	Segregate from OR / KEEP APART	Segregate from
2.2 Non-flammable /non-toxic	2 (Compressed gas)	KEEP APART		KEEP APART	KEEP APART
2.3 Toxic	2 (Toxic gas)	Segregate from OR / KEEP APART	KEEP APART		Segregate from
FLAMMABLE LIQUIDS	3 (Flammable liquid)	Segregate from	KEEP APART	Segregate from	
FLAMMABLE SOLIDS 4.1 Readily combustible	4 (Flammable solid)	Segregate from	Separation may not be necessary	KEEP APART	KEEP APART
4.2 Spontaneously combustible	4 (Spontaneously combustible)	Segregate from	Segregate from	Segregate from	Segregate from
4.3 Dangerous when wet	4 (Dangerous when wet)	Segregate from	Separation may not be necessary	KEEP APART	Segregate from
OXIDISING SUBSTANCES 5.1 Oxidising substances	5 (Oxidising agent 5.1)	Segregate from	Separation may not be necessary	Separation may not be necessary	Segregate from
5.2 Organic peroxides	5 (Organic peroxide 5.2)	ISOLATE	Segregate from	Segregate from	ISOLATE
TOXIC SUBSTANCES	6 (Toxic)	KEEP APART	Separation may not be necessary	Separation may not be necessary	KEEP APART
CORROSIVE SUBSTANCES	8 (Corrosive)	KEEP APART	KEEP APART	KEEP APART	KEEP APART

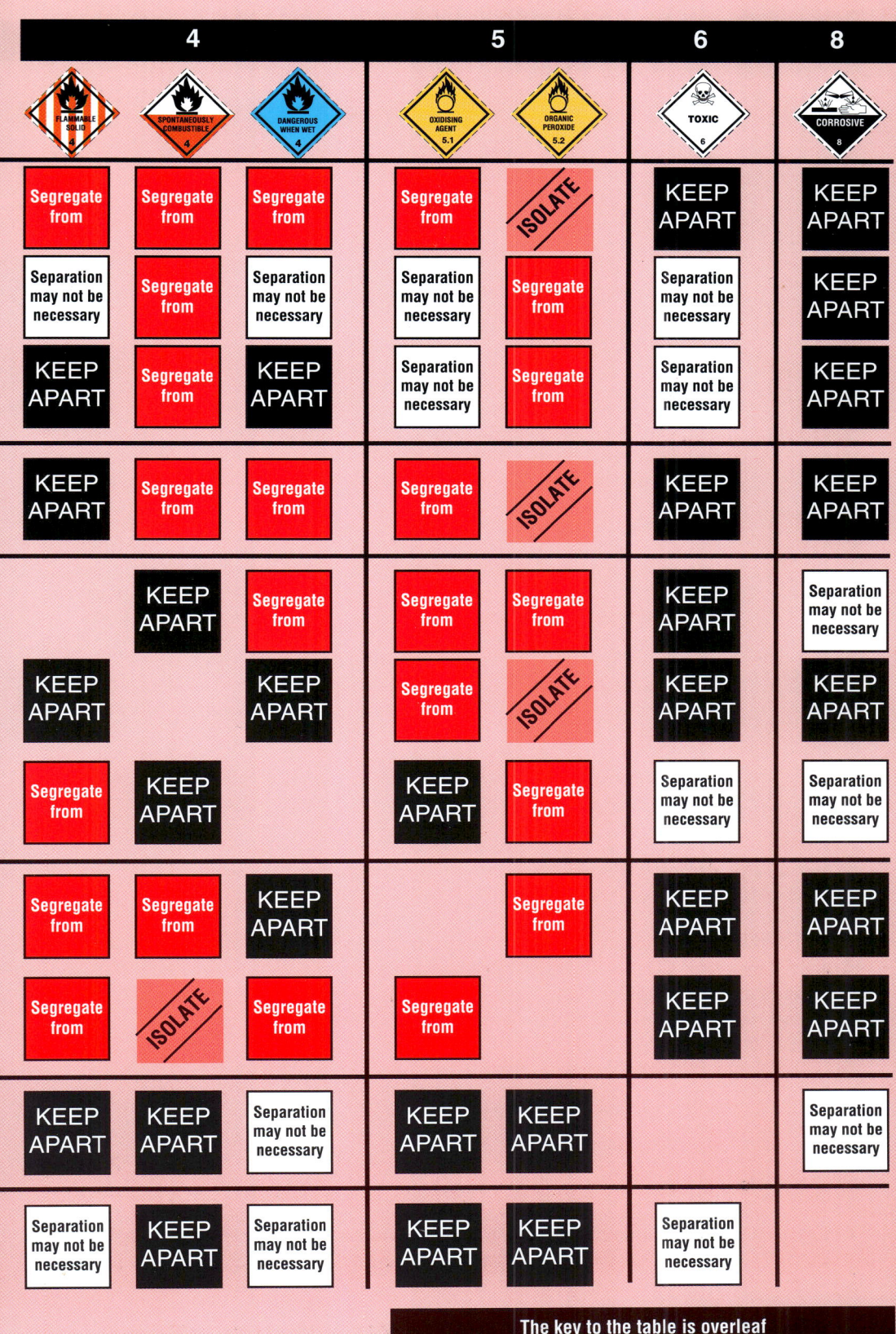

The key to the table is overleaf

Table 1 Separation and segregation of dangerous substances (previous page)

Key

Separation may not be necessary, but suppliers should be consulted about requirements for individual substances. In particular, it should be noted that some types of chemicals within the same class, particularly Class 8 corrosives may react violently, generate a lot of heat if mixed or evolve toxic fumes.

Separate packages by at least 3 metres or one gangway width, whichever is the greater distance, in the storeroom or storage area outdoors. Materials in non-combustible packaging which are not dangerous substances and which present a low fire hazard may be stored in the separation area. This standard of separation should be regarded as a minimum between substances known to react together readily, if that reaction would increase the danger of an escalating incident.

These combinations should not be kept in the same building compartment or outdoor storage compound. Compartment walls should be imperforate, of at least 30 minutes fire resistance and sufficiently durable to withstand normal wear and tear. Brick or concrete construction is recommended. An alternative is to provide separate outdoor storage compounds with an adequate space between them.

This is used for organic peroxides, for which dedicated buildings are recommended. Alternatively, some peroxides may be stored outside in fire-resisting secure cabinets. In either case, adequate separation from other buildings and boundaries is required.

* The lower standard refers to the outside storage of gas cylinders. Where non-liquefied flammable gases are concerned the 3 metres separation distance may be reduced to 1 metre.[31]

Where a particular material has the properties of more than one class, the classification giving the more onerous segregation requirements should be used.

71   Following the guidance in Table 1 will not necessarily achieve safe storage conditions. You need to consult the material safety data sheets for reactivity data to determine whether the substances are incompatible. Many corrosive substances in Class 8 are incompatible. These may react together to produce heat or toxic gases. Examples are:

(a)   acids/hypochlorites - generate chlorine gas;

(b)   acids/cyanides - generate hydrogen cyanide gas;

(c)   acids/alkalis - generate heat;

(d)   acids/sulphides - generate hydrogen sulphide.

Generally, the segregation of acids from other substances will go some way to ensuring incompatible substances are not stored together. The extent of such incompatibility problems is reduced because damage to two packages must occur before any reaction can take place. Also, mixing and reaction is likely to be slow if both incompatible components are solids.

72   The miscellaneous dangerous substances in Class 9 and the other dangerous substances in the carriage Regulations[4] have quite varied properties, and no general advice can be given regarding segregation. You need to obtain this advice from the supplier.

73   Following your assessment of the hazard of the material, you are now able to decide where the material should be physically stored. The next section of this book covers the general precautions associated with the location and design of storage areas and buildings.

Warehouse or outdoor storage compound location

74   If you are considering the location for a new warehouse or outdoor storage compound for storing dangerous substances, then part of your risk assessment will consider, in the case of an incident, the effect of the substances on neighbouring property or populations. Certain sectors of the population are considered vulnerable, for example schools, hospitals or retirement homes.

75   If you are already operating at existing premises, your risk assessment will help you decide the quantities or types of materials which can be stored so as not to impose a significant risk on neighbouring populations.

76   The location of new buildings with respect to boundaries is controlled under building regulations[32,33] administered by the local authority. While the specified separation distances reduce the likelihood of fire spreading to neighbouring property, they do not take account of the higher levels of thermal radiation which occur with certain highly flammable materials. Existing guidance[34-39] gives separation distances for some of these materials. These will be typically greater than those required under the Building Regulations. In every case, the greater separation distance should be adopted.

Means of access

77   There are many different designs and locations of warehouses or outdoor storage compounds. However, in all cases, access to the storage area is necessary for the carrying out of the various operations. The standards applicable for new buildings are covered in guidance[40] made under the Building Regulations.[32,33]

78   You should also remember that access is important in emergency situations. The access to the store needs to be adequate for the rapid deployment of any additional fire-fighting equipment by the local fire brigade. If the conditions on site are congested, you may need to consider traffic movement schemes, for example speed restrictions and one-way systems.

79   Obviously, access for the fire brigade during an incident is paramount and hence this access should be available at all times. If access of unauthorised vehicles is allowed or parking is not controlled, then access may not be possible. These aspects will have been discussed already prior to granting planning permission for new buildings.

Means of escape in case of fire

80   Just as important as access to the warehouse or storage compound are escape routes from the stores for use in an emergency, particularly involving fire. The underlying principle of a means of escape is to ensure that people do not become trapped by fire, and this is most readily achieved by the provision of two independent routes to safety from the store. From any point in the store, the question to ask yourself is: 'If a fire occurred here, could I turn my back on the fire and escape to a place of safety?' If the answer to the question is 'No', then you need to consider providing alternatives which may involve the installation of additional means of escape.

81   The means of escape in case of fire should be discussed with the fire authority.[41] Once the routes are determined, they need to be maintained so they can be used at all necessary times. To achieve these aims the means of escape should be kept clear of obstructions and, if the store is used at night, adequately illuminated. Emergency lighting may be required as back-up to the normal lighting.

Containment of the hazard

Building construction

82   Storage buildings and outdoor storage compounds for dangerous substances are subject to controls under building and planning legislation. In England and Wales an approved document[40] sets out standards for fire resistance and compartment size for industrial or storage buildings. The use classes take no account of the specific hazards of the materials being stored, and in some cases, where large quantities of dangerous substances are involved, different or higher standards may be appropriate.

83   In Scotland the building standards[33] are different. A use category specific to the storage of certain types of dangerous substance is given and more rigorous requirements are imposed.

84   In both cases, the Regulations specify standards for fire resistance, compartment size and also means of escape and assistance to the fire brigade.

85   Buildings for storing dangerous substances should preferably be constructed of non-combustible materials. Fire-resisting external walls provide some protection against an external fire that may be started deliberately. Where the Highly Flammable Liquids and Liquefied Petroleum Gases Regulations 1972[6] apply, there may be specific requirements for the fire resistance of the building.

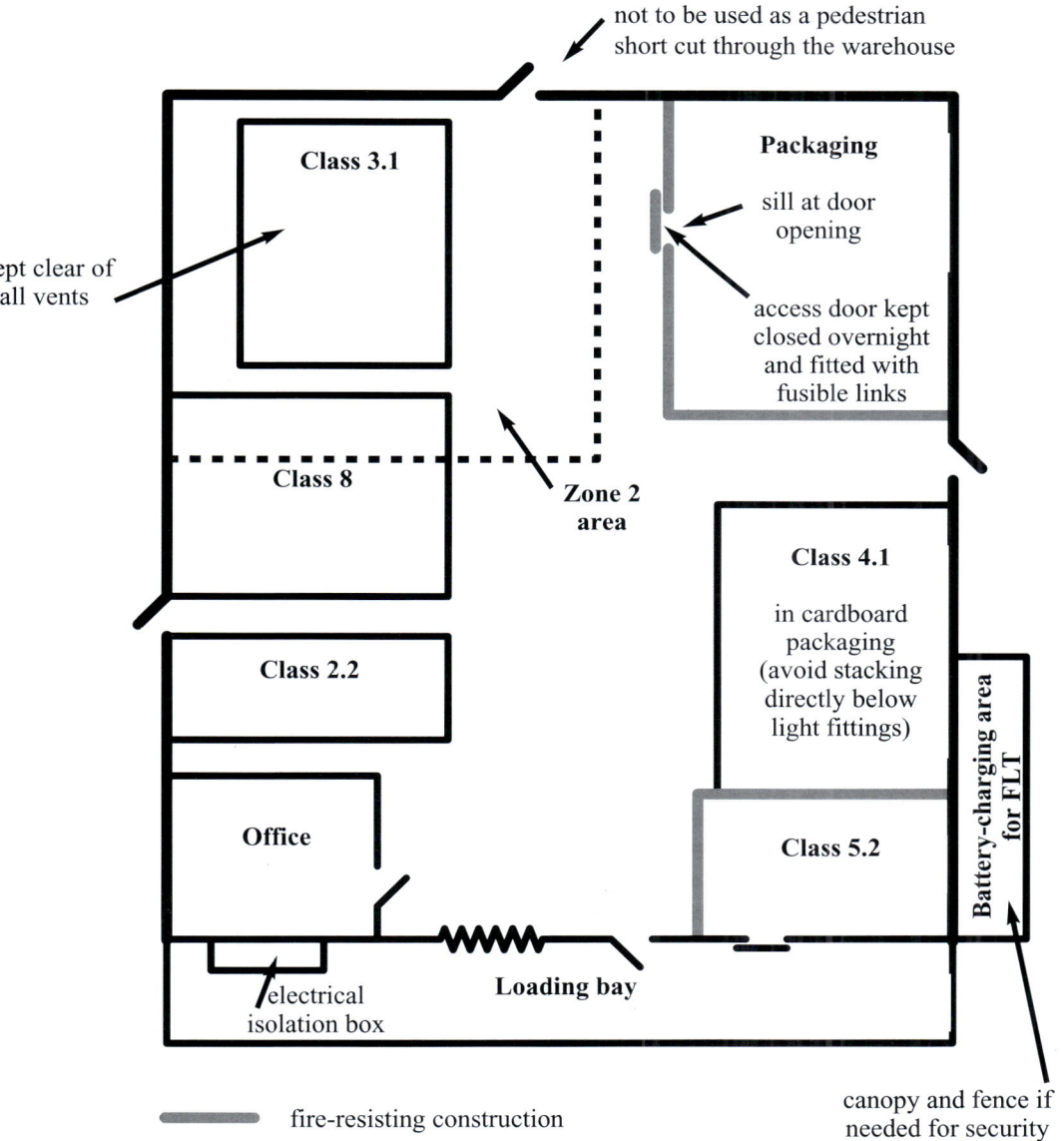

not to be used as a pedestrian
short cut through the warehouse

Packaging

Class 3.1

sill at door
opening

ept clear of
all vents

access door kept
closed overnight
and fitted with
fusible links

Class 8

**Zone 2
area**

Class 4.1

in cardboard
packaging
(avoid stacking
directly below
light fittings)

Class 2.2

Battery-charging area
for FLT

Office

Class 5.2

electrical
isolation box

Loading bay

canopy and fence if
needed for security

fire-resisting construction

Figure 2 Example of good warehouse layout

86   The standards of fire resistance required under health and safety legislation are intended to allow sufficient time, in the event of a fire, for the alarm to be raised, for people to escape, and for fire fighting to be put safely in hand. The standards of structural fire resistance are determined by the local authority building control department via the building regulations, or standards. Insurers of your premises may also have requirements for structural fire protection and separation, fire suppression systems and fire compartmentation.

87   The building regulations may require higher standards, as they also cover the spread of fire throughout a building, or from building to building.

88   In designing storage buildings you need to consider the layout of storage within the warehouse. Some warehouses have an inbuilt store within the main warehouse. This interior store may be used to store particular hazardous materials, for example highly flammable liquids and gases, or peroxides, and so the store is required to be fire resisting. Obviously some access into this interior store will be required (see Figure 2).

89   It is better if access to the interior store is available from outside the main store. This is beneficial as the fire resistance, between the main store and the interior store, is not being jeopardised by any access doors being permanently left open. Alternatively the access doors to the interior store may be linked to the fire alarm. Activation of the fire alarm system should result in closure of the fire access doors. It is better to close internal fire doors manually at the end of the working day, rather than depend on the automatic closure devices.

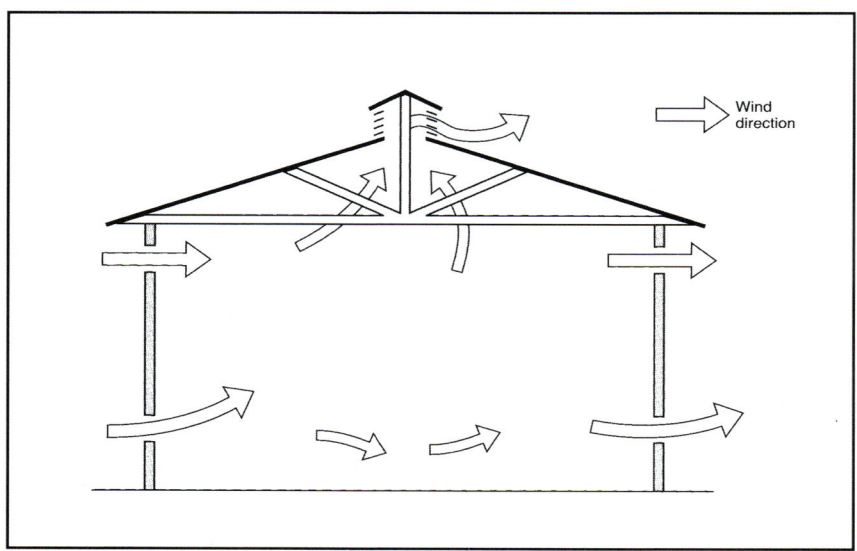

Figure 3 Roof and wall vents together give good natural ventilation

90   To prevent dangerous concentrations of flammable vapours building up within the store as the result of a leak of a highly flammable liquid or gas, the store needs to be adequately ventilated (see Figure 3). The simplest method of ensuring adequate ventilation at all relevant times is to provide fixed, permanent openings (such as air bricks or louvers) in external walls at high and low levels. If openings are only provided on two walls, a cross flow induced by wind forces is encouraged. Similarly, openings at high and low levels will encourage air circulation by thermal currents. Vehicle access doors may provide sufficient ventilation during the working day, but you need to consider in your risk assessment the ventilation requirements during out-of-hours. Specific advice for flammable liquids and LPG is given elsewhere.[35,36]

91   Large buildings may require mechanical ventilation to achieve an adequate air movement. Where this is necessary, the mechanical ventilation needs to operate constantly. Failure of the ventilation system can be detected by the use of an air flow monitoring device, installed in the ventilation ductwork (such as a flow switch or differential pressure switch) and linked to an alarm. In cases of doubt, measurements may be made of the air change rate actually achieved in a completed building. A competent ventilation engineer should be able to do this.

Design and construction of containers

92   The main protection against the dangers arising from the storage of dangerous substances in containers is the integrity of the packaging. Individual containers may leak, break or puncture, causing a small escape of material, and so arrangements need to be in place to deal with these situations.

93   Both the Chemicals (Hazard Information and Packaging for Supply) Regulations[5] and the Carriage of Dangerous Goods (Classification, Packaging and Labelling) and Use of Transportable Pressure Receptacles Regulations 1996[4] require manufacturers, suppliers and distributors to ensure that chemicals are packaged safely.

94   All containers should be designed and constructed to standards suitable for the purpose. They should be robust and have well-fitting lids or tops to resist spillage if knocked over. There are specific standards available for containers and packagings to comply with transport legislation. Containers need to be of an appropriate UN Performance Tested type. Such containers are suitable also for storage conditions.

95   Where necessary, containers should be protected against corrosion (for example by painting) and against degradation by light, particularly for plastic containers (by suitable shading). In addition, the material from which the containers are made needs to be compatible with the chemical and physical properties of the contents to ensure that no interaction occurs which might cause leakage.

Figure 4 Protected fork-lift truck

96   If containers are reused, such as for storing process waste, they should be individually inspected for damage before refilling and marked as such. Problems commonly arise from damaged linings to drums, or from corrosion occurring near to the base seams of drums.

Handling and transport

97   Containers need to be stacked in a safe manner which facilitates handling operations. The stack design should allow any leaking container to be quickly spotted, easily removed and appropriately dealt with. With 205-litre metal drums and similar containers, they are normally stacked no more than four high and preferably on pallets. Drums stored on their sides need to be prevented from moving by suitable chocks. Containers must not be stacked so as to obstruct ventilation openings or means of escape in case of fire.

98   You need to ensure that the most appropriate mechanical handling equipment is used (see Figure 4). This is clearly dependent on the types of packages encountered. Improvised arrangements for the movement of packages may lead to accidents, damaged packaging and spillage of the contents. Palletised goods need to be made secure to prevent accidental movement during the handling operations.

99   Vehicles containing packaged dangerous goods need to be parked in a safe place during loading or unloading. Access to and from the site, and to particular storage buildings or compounds, needs to be considered. Your risk assessment will also need to consider the possibility of a collision with a vehicle which may result in the spillage of dangerous goods. Where separation distances to a premise boundary apply to permanent storage compounds, you are recommended to maintain these distances wherever possible. For instance, avoid parking loaded vehicles in these areas for extended periods.

Operations

100   The store should not be used for activities where spillages are more likely, for example dispensing, mixing and repacking. Such operations should be carried out in a separate area, and in a way which reduces spills and dangerous releases. The risk from such operations is greatest with flammable materials, particularly liquids. In these cases, operations need to be carried out within a fire-resisting enclosure which is suitably bunded to contain any spillages. This control measure should allow some protection against a fire in the operations area spreading to involve stored goods.

101   You need to make sure that any racking installed is properly constructed, stable and adequately maintained, and that the maximum loading is not exceeded. Consider how you can load the racking to avoid the generation of unstable stacks, for example by loading empty racks from the bottom up. Your risk assessment needs to consider the movement of vehicles in the store. The supports and racking structure may require protection against impact from vehicles.

102   Some warehouses are not racked and goods are simply stored in 'block stacks'. Consequently stack sizes may need to be limited to restrict the severity of any fire. In these cases you should set standards for the maximum stack size and height. Stacking heights should be limited so that the lowest layer of packages will not be overloaded and the stability of the pile not endangered. You can get advice on stacking heights from the supplier of the material.

Spillage control

General

103   It is important to have means of controlling spillages and releases within the storage area to prevent the uncontrolled spread of liquids. A number of control measures are possible. You can provide sand bags, absorbent granules or other means for the clearing up of small spills. Contaminated granules etc will need to be disposed of safely and appropriately by the use of a licensed waste disposal contractor. For this, you should provide a number of spare clean empty bags or drums. Proprietary salvage containers are available to hold leaking drums etc. You will need to correctly label the used spare bags or salvage containers accordingly.

Control of spillages in outdoor storage areas

104   To contain spillages in outdoor storage areas, an impervious sill or low bund can be installed. This should enclose a volume which is at least 110% of the capacity of the largest container. Ramps can be provided over the sill to allow for the access of fork lift trucks, pallet trucks etc into the storage area.

105   The surface of the storage area needs to be impervious and slightly sloped so that any liquid spilt from the containers can flow away to a safe contained place. An alternative method to using a bund is to direct spillages of liquid to another area. This could be to an evaporation

area (either within the storage area or separated from it), or via drainage to a remote sump, interceptor or separator. Corrosion of the base of a container can result in potential leakage of the contents. Good drainage of surface rain water away from the containers, or the storage of containers on pallets, can reduce the likelihood of this corrosion. Depending on the hazards of the materials stored, it may be necessary to incorporate an interceptor pit in the site drains, so that small spillages can be retained on site.

106   Combustible materials (including weed growth) need to be excluded from the area surrounding the sill or bund, as their presence increases the fire risk. One metre is considered adequate. If weed growth is controlled by the use of weedkillers, you should not use oxidising agents, eg those which contain sodium chlorate.

Control of spillage in buildings

107   Storage rooms or buildings should have floors constructed of materials that are resistant to and compatible with the materials stored. For instance many acids attack concrete floors, solvents attack bitumen floors, and timber floors impregnated by flammable liquids are an increased fire risk. Containment of any leaks or releases from containers can be achieved by either sloping the floor away from the door, or by providing a sill across the door opening. Typically, such sills are about 150 mm high, and again ramps might be required to allow access for wheeled trolleys, fork-lift trucks etc. Some additional containment may be required if the building's drains link to the site drainage systems (see paragraph 105).

108   You need to remember that the arrangement of spillage containment/drainage in buildings must consider material segregation. Liquid spillages should be prevented from running into areas where incompatible materials are stored. This may be achieved in warehouses by installing internal bunded areas, in-rack bunds or drip trays under each pallet and connected to an appropriate drainage system.

109   Containment and spillage control also needs to take account of the presence of any fire suppression systems. Some lighter than water materials can be spread by floating on water with such systems. The spillage control should be adequate to cope with the use of the installed fire suppression systems. Internal fire doors are unlikely to prevent the spread of fire from an expanding liquid pool unless sills or appropriate drainage arrangements have been provided at the door opening.

110   These requirements should not be confused with the fire-fighting water run-off containment (see section on Controls for off-site risks, paragraphs 161-164) that may be required to prevent the release of materials from the storage area to the environment, in the event of an incident. Such run-off containment may need to take account of water that may be applied from both installed systems and manual fire fighting.

Security

111   Physical control measures can minimise the risks of fire or explosion, but these can be defeated if trespassing or tampering, deliberate or otherwise, is allowed to take place. So your security arrangements, both during the working day and outside normal hours, need to consider the possibility of arson and vandalism. During the working day it should not be possible for an unauthorised person to enter the storage area unchallenged. One way of achieving this is to keep the storage area locked, with access to the keys being restricted to authorised people.

112   The standard of security required will depend, among other factors, on the consequences of a major fire. Intruder alarms, security patrols etc may be considered appropriate, but you should not forget the other simple precautions that can be taken, such as maintaining fences and external walls. Broken windows and missing construction panels and sheets should be fixed. It is through openings of this type that fires can be deliberately started or unauthorised entry into the store can occur. Stacks of pallets or empty drums up against the building may assist unauthorised access, and they can also act as the fuel source for an arsonist.

113   Where security fencing is installed around the storage area, its design needs to take full account of the general fire precautions required.

Precautions against ignition

114   There are many possible sources of ignition in most storage buildings (see Figure 5). These include:

(a)   smoking and smokers' materials;

(b)   maintenance work, particularly involving hot work;

(c)   electrical power supplies;

(d)   storage close to hot pipes or light fittings;

(e)   arson;

(f)   heating systems incorporating open flames;

(g)   warehouse vehicles, and battery charging facilities;

(h)   LPG fuelled shrink-wrapping machines.

You need to ensure control is maintained over all potential sources of ignition at sites storing dangerous substances. Some examples of the precautions that can be taken are given in the following paragraphs.

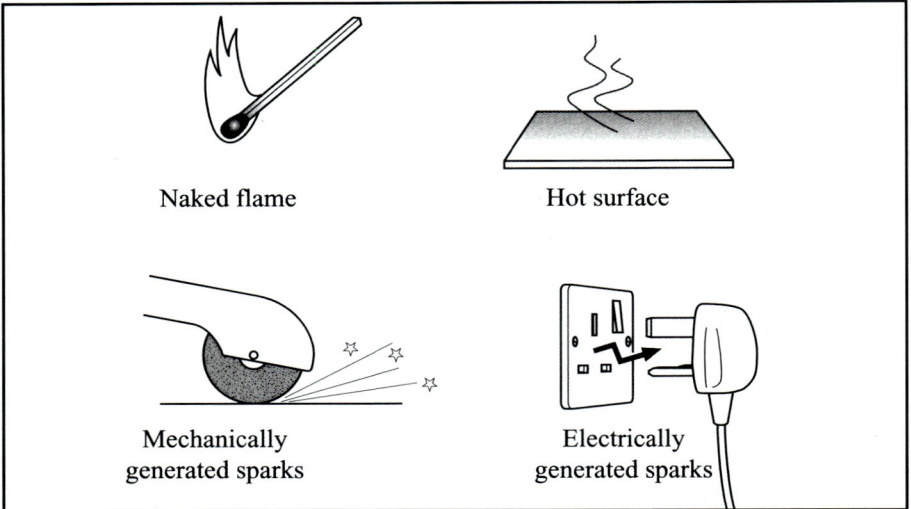

Figure 5 Potential forms of ignition

Naked flame

Hot surface

Mechanically generated sparks

Electrically generated sparks

Smoking

115   Smoking and smokers' materials have caused many fires. You should prohibit smoking in the actual storage areas, and provide designated areas either in separate non-storage buildings, or in a room separated from the store by fire-resisting walls, doors and windows. You need to make visitors to the store aware of, and comply with, the smoking rules on site.

Hot work

116   A permit-to-work system should be used to control any hot work.

117   Precautions to be taken before, during and after the work include:

(a)   clearing, as far as is reasonably practicable, all flammable or combustible materials away from the work area;

(b)   checking for combustible material on one side of a partition or wall when work is to take place on the other side;

(c)   having suitable fire extinguishers at hand and maintaining a careful watch for fire during the work;

(d)   protecting combustible material that cannot be cleared by providing suitable screens or partitions;

(e)   examining the area thoroughly for some time after the work has finished to make sure there is no smouldering material present;

(f)   as a sensible precaution, stopping all hot work by a safe period before the end of the working day.

Burning or welding work at high level is particularly hazardous as hot fragments may travel a considerable distance and still be capable of igniting flammable or heat-sensitive materials.

Electrical equipment

118   The Electricity at Work Regulations 1989[42] require any electrical equipment, fixed or portable, to be correctly maintained. For new storage facilities it would be good practice to install main switch and distribution boards in a separate fire-resisting room, located at the main store entrance, or preferably accessible directly from the outside.

119   If electrical equipment items are installed within the store, for example lighting, then you need to ensure that easily ignitable materials are not stored close to them. Similarly, power cables should be kept clear of any area where they might be attacked by a leak of corrosive substance.

120   It is good practice to turn off all non-essential electrical equipment, preferably at the main isolation switch, outside normal working hours and when the store is unoccupied for long periods of time.

121   Where possible, electrical equipment should be located in non-hazardous areas. When there are stored substances, that give off flammable vapours if the packaging opens or breaks, a hazardous area classification exercise should be carried out to assess the extent of any such areas.

122   Hazardous area classification is discussed in a number of publications.[43,44] The concept of hazardous area classification has, in the past, been used solely as the basis for selecting fixed electrical equipment. However, it can also be used to help eliminate potential ignition sources, including portable electrical equipment, vehicles and hot surfaces, from flammable atmospheres. Where only storage of packaged dangerous goods is undertaken, there should not normally be any need to classify an area as more hazardous than zone 2.

123   If electrical equipment needs to be located in a hazardous environment, it should be constructed or protected so as to prevent danger. This is a requirement of the Electricity at Work Regulations 1989[42] and can be achieved by selecting equipment built to an explosion-protected standard (ie an appropriate British Standard or equivalent). Advice on selecting, installing and maintaining explosion-protected electrical equipment is given in BS EN 60079-14[45] and in a short guide published by the Institution of Chemical Engineers.[46]

124   There are also regulations which apply to both electrical and non-electrical equipment, the Equipment and Protective Systems Intended for Use in Potentially Explosive Atmospheres Regulations 1996.[47] However, they are aimed at manufacturers and suppliers, requiring them to ensure the equipment is safe. Such equipment should carry CE marking. From July 2003 you will have to select CE-marked equipment but, until then, you can select new equipment that does not carry CE marking provided it is safe.

125   It is recommended that you control the use of unauthorised electrical equipment, such as radios, heaters or kettles, in the store. There have been instances when this type of equipment has caused a fire. Such equipment is normally brought into the store from employees' homes once its use at home has ceased. It is likely therefore to be old and in a state of poor repair, and will not have been maintained.

Protection of vehicles

126   Vehicles which have to operate within the hazardous areas in storage buildings or areas need to be protected to an appropriate standard, to avoid ignition of any flammable vapours. The HSE guidance publication HSG113[48] provides further advice on the use and protection of lift trucks.

127   Preferably, LPG and petrol engined vehicles should not be parked in the storage area outside normal working hours. Recharging batteries generates hydrogen, a flammable gas. Consequently the recharging of electric powered vehicles, such as fork lift trucks, should be done in a bay separate from the store. The type of bay necessary will depend on the risk associated with the materials being stored.

Heating systems

128   Occasionally storage buildings or internal stores containing dangerous goods are heated. In this case the heating system should not be an ignition source. The use solely of indirect heating can achieve this. Examples include radiators fed remotely by hot water pipes, or indirectly fired gas or oil appliances (ie those which take the air for combustion from a safe place and exhaust the products of combustion to the outside air). Electrically heated radiators which comply with BS EN 60079-14[45] may be used. In all cases the heating system should be protected against the build-up of flammable residues on hot surfaces.

Shrink-wrapping operations

129   Ideally, heat shrink-wrapping operations should not be carried out in the store. They should take place either in a separate building or in a specifically designed bay within the building. The type of bay necessary will depend on the risk associated with the materials in store and those being wrapped. Stretch-wrapping is much preferred to heat shrink-wrapping as the risk of fire is greatly reduced. There are few occasions where it cannot replace the latter.

FIRE PRECAUTIONS AND EMERGENCY PROCEDURES

Fire precautions

Introduction

130   Much can be done to prevent fire, and following the advice in this book should greatly reduce the chances of it occurring. Unfortunately the possibility of a fire always remains. It is therefore important for you to have in place a pre-planned response to such emergencies, including the appropriate actions to be taken in the event of a fire and efficient arrangements for calling the fire brigade.

General fire precautions

131   If a fire occurs people need to be able to quickly escape from its effects and reach a place of safety. The term 'general fire precautions' (GFP) is used to describe the structural features and equipment provided to achieve this aim. It covers:

(a)   escape routes to fire exits;

(b)   fire-fighting equipment;

(c)   a system of giving warning in the event of fire;

(d)   an efficient arrangement for calling the fire brigade; and

(e)   management procedures to ensure that all of the above are available and maintained, and that there is adequate training in their use.

Detailed consideration of these topics is outside the scope of this book, although some mention has been made earlier concerning the means of escape in case of fire. In the majority of circumstances, the requirements for adequate GFPs are made under the Fire Precautions Act 1971[49] and the Fire Precautions (Workplace) Regulations 1997.[41] For advice on these matters the fire authority must be consulted.

Fire-fighting equipment

132   An adequate number of fire extinguishers should be present within the storage area. Their primary purpose is to tackle incipient fires, which often do not involve the dangerous goods, thereby reducing the risk to people and enabling them to make their escape. Anybody expected to use a fire extinguisher should be properly trained. With some types of dangerous substances any attempt to fight a fire may be unwise, but the ability to a tackle a waste bin or small packaging fire might prevent a serious incident occurring.

133   The extinguishers need to be positioned in conspicuous locations along the escape routes, such that nobody in the storage area needs to travel more than 30 metres to reach one. Unless the location of an extinguisher is self-evident, its position needs to be identified by appropriate safety signs. Such signs should comply with the Health and Safety (Safety Signs and Signals) Regulations 1996[50] or BS 5499: Part 1.[51]

134   To reduce the risk of corrosion, it is sensible to keep extinguishers off the ground and to provide protection against the weather.

135   Extinguishers should be to a recognised standard such as BS EN 3[52] or BS 5423 and be suitable for tackling fires involving the dangerous substances stored. BS 5423 has now been withdrawn. All new extinguishers should comply with BS EN 3[52] but existing extinguishers complying with BS 5423 are still acceptable if already in situ and remaining serviceable. You should seek the advice and guidance of the fire authority and/or equipment supplier on the type and size of fire extinguishers required.

136   There should be an effective means of both raising the alarm and giving warning in case of fire in the storage area. It should be audible to all those likely to be affected by the fire. This may vary from small storage areas, where a shout of 'fire' might suffice, to larger areas where a klaxon or siren might be required. You need to discuss your requirements with the fire authority who will advise on appropriate systems.

137   An assembly point should be identified for people evacuating from such areas, so that they can be accounted for. It should be safe from the effects of fire and smoke. Careful consideration is needed if the smoke can be particularly toxic, for example with fires in pesticide stores. In these cases, the assembly point may be on an alternative site or within another building.

Fire protection

138   Measures such as compartmentation (ie the storage of the packaged dangerous substances in a fire-resistant enclosure) can limit the spread of fire and restrict damage to a specific area. The duration of the protection will depend on the notional period of fire resistance of the enclosure. So if you decide to use this method, the required period of fire resistance will need to be determined. Such determination will depend on a variety of factors

including the anticipated fire load and duration, and the time for the fire brigade to arrive and start tackling the fire.

Fire detection

139   Outside working hours, or in warehouses which are empty of people for long periods, any outbreak of fire could develop unseen. This could pose a risk to people, both on and off-site, perhaps from smoke containing significant quantities of toxic materials. Consequently it may require a means of providing early detection of the fire. This may be achieved by installing automatic fire detectors which will trigger an alarm, alerting those on site to the fire. They will also, as necessary, warn those in the surrounding area and summon the fire brigade. Advice on the selection and installation of suitable equipment is given in BS 5839,[53] where it is recommended that the work is carried out by a fire protection engineer who is experienced in the installation of such systems. Again, advice may be obtained from the fire authority.

Fire suppression systems

140   By tackling a fire almost as soon as it is detected, automatic fire suppression systems can be of value in significantly reducing both the risk and damage the fire would otherwise pose, if left to develop unchallenged.

141   Where fire suppression systems are installed, it is important, especially in those warehouses where the materials stored frequently change, to ensure the system is appropriate for those contents.

142   The most commonly encountered system is the automatic sprinkler installation. Typically using water as the extinguishing medium, there are two basic types:

(a) Sealed sprinkler head system

In this system each sprinkler head is sealed with a temperature-sensitive device, for example, a fusible link or glass bulb. As such, the only devices which operate are those which become sufficiently heated, ie those in the vicinity of the fire. This then limits the discharge of water to that area. These systems are ideal for controlling fires in materials that can be 'wetted', ie absorb water. Also by limiting water discharge to the area of the fire, water damage to stock is reduced and the size of the containment system needed to prevent fire water run-off is minimised.

(b) Open deluge system

The system is linked to an appropriate fire detection system where, when a fire is detected, water is immediately discharged over an entire area. The purpose of this is to 'wet' and cool not only the materials involved in the fire, but also anything close by which might otherwise become involved. Such systems are useful against fires involving highly flammable materials, that might be difficult or impossible to extinguish once ignited.

143   You should note that fires involving flammable liquids, especially those immiscible in water, are unlikely to be controlled by water alone. Indeed it may cause the fire to spread. In some circumstances the use of fire-fighting foam with a sprinkler system will provide effective protection for stocks of flammable liquid. Foam may not, however, be effective on 'running fires', for example fires in high-racked stores of flammable liquids in plastic containers.

144   Automatic fire suppression systems should be designed and installed to a required standard, such as BS 5306: Part 2.[54] However, care must be taken in using the commodity classification scheme within the standard. Palletised stocks of flammable liquids in plastic containers should be classified as an 'oil and flammable liquid hazard' rather than 'flammable liquids in combustible containers'. As with all systems required to work on demand, it is imperative that they are correctly maintained and serviced. This is especially true with, for example, a suppression system which will rarely, if ever, be used,

Smoke control systems

145   The discharge of smoke from a building in the early stages of a fire can not only help protect the means of escape, but it can assist the fire brigade in their fire-fighting operations and delay lateral fire spread.

146   The ideal smoke control systems are purpose-designed for the building and the materials stored in it. There are essentially two types: natural ventilation using opening vents; or a powered exhaust system which operates at a specified temperature.

147   Roof lights made from materials with a low melting point, providing they are of sufficient area, can also provide effective smoke control. They can however drip molten plastic into the building, escalating the fire by acting as a source of ignition or affecting the operation of sprinkler heads. It is unlikely that they can be made to operate as early in a fire as a purpose-designed system, which is the preferred option.

148   Where a separate fire detection system, or a fire suppression system, is installed, it is important to ensure that these operate before the smoke control system does. The interaction of smoke control systems and fire suppression systems is a complex matter, and the combined system needs to be designed and installed by competent fire protection engineers.

149   Guidance is available on the design of smoke ventilation systems.[55]

Emergency procedures

150   Initiating emergency procedures at the earliest stage of an incident can significantly reduce the impact on people and premises.

151   You need to develop a procedure for dealing with emergencies. Consideration needs to be given to the range of possible events, taking into account the following:

(a)   the nature and quantities of the dangerous substances stored;

(b)   the location of the storage facility and its design; and

(c)   the people, both on-site and off-site who may be affected.

152   You may have a storage area in which any incident is likely to be confined to that area, or to the building containing the store. In this case the emergency procedures may be limited to ensuring that everyone can safely escape from the effects of a fire or toxic gas release, and that the fire brigade is called with minimum delay.

153   The fire brigade has duties under the Fire Services Act 1947[56] to enable it to tackle any outbreak of fire. This includes familiarising itself with the means of access to premises and the layout, including the availability of water supplies. To assist in this, the following should be agreed with the fire authority:

(a)   the provision and maintenance of suitable access for fire-fighting personnel and their vehicles; and

(b)   as necessary, the provision of a convenient fire main and hydrant.

154   Where there is a possibility that a fire in the store might spread to affect other parts, whether on-site or off-site, you need to consider how the risk to anyone present can be reduced. Similarly, if a fire could reach the store, preventive measures have to be considered.

155   Clearly, where you conclude that precautions are needed, in consultation with the fire authority, the extent of them will depend on the nature of the site. They could vary from housing suitable fire extinguishers or fire hose reels to tackle an incipient fire to installing sprinkler systems.

156   People expected to use the equipment need to be trained and rehearsed in how to do so, without exposing themselves or others to any unnecessary risk from the fire. This needs to be discussed with the fire authority.

157   The fire brigade when they arrive will assume responsibility for fire-fighting operations. It is therefore important that they are aware of the fire-fighting equipment and capability on site. This includes having in place agreed procedures with the works fire team, if there is one, to ensure that control of the incident is maintained and that nobody is exposed to unnecessary risk during handover. Any subsequent role for the works fire team should be agreed with the fire authority and detailed in your emergency procedures.

158   It is recommended that, where a number of different types of dangerous substances are stored, a comprehensive record of the stock is readily available. This record would provide details of the quantity and exact location of all the dangerous substances in the store. The record would require updating each time a stock movement occurred or at the end of the working day. A copy of the record needs to be available at a point on the site which is unlikely to be affected by an emergency, so it can be used by both management and the emergency services when dealing with an incident.

159   Where 25 tonnes or more of dangerous substances are stored, the Dangerous Substances (Notification and Marking of Sites) Regulations 1990[57] will apply. These Regulations make specific requirements for posting hazard warning signs and for the design of the signs to be used. You should consult the fire brigade about their requirements for the actual siting of the signs.

160   It would be useful if the emergency services were given an out-of-hours telephone contact number, so that they can obtain specialist advice when dealing with an incident.

Controls for off-site risks

161   Fire water run-off may place a major strain on normal drainage facilities. Interceptors or special drainage schemes may be necessary, particularly at large installations, to minimise the risk of contaminating local water courses. Consultation with the Environment Agency (or in Scotland, the SEPA) and the fire authority may be appropriate.

162   Guidance on this topic can be found in the HSE guidance note EH70[58] and in a document published by the Construction Industry Research and Information Association.[59]

163   Where foreseeable incidents may affect people or property beyond the site boundary, the emergency services should be consulted when preparing the emergency procedures.

164   Formal on-site and off-site emergency plans are required at sites subject to regulations 7 to 12 of the Control of Industrial Major Accident Hazard Regulations 1984 (CIMAH)[23] - see HSE guidance publications HSG25[60] and HSR21.[26]

APPENDIX 1: LEGAL REQUIREMENTS

Introduction

1　It is a legal requirement under health and safety law that those responsible for work activities ensure that :

(a)　hazards are adequately identified;

(b)　risks are adequately assessed; and

(c)　suitable control measures are put into practice.

2　Measures must be taken to eliminate or control the risks unless doing so involves a sacrifice (time, trouble or cost) which is grossly disproportionate to the level of risk. However, the ability to pay for additional control measures is not a deciding factor as to whether they are necessary. Where it is not possible to remove the risk then the arrangements for managing the activity safely are particularly important.

3　The next section in this book gives information on the main health and safety regulations concerning the storage of packaged dangerous substances.

Carriage of Dangerous Goods (Classification, Packaging and Labelling) and Use of Transportable Pressure Receptacles Regulations 1996[4]

4　These Regulations apply to the transportation of dangerous goods by road and rail. Their aim is to reduce the risks involved in transporting such substances by requiring them to be correctly classified, packaged and labelled according to that classification.

5　They specify that dangerous goods should be carried in suitable receptacles which will not leak under normal handling. These should bear appropriate warning labels giving information on the nature of the hazards.

6   Two associated documents, the *Approved carriage list*[61] and the *Approved requirements and test methods for the classification and packaging of dangerous goods for carriage*[62] provide assistance to enable compliance with these Regulations.

The Carriage of Dangerous Goods by Road 1996[63] and the Carriage of Dangerous Goods by Rail Regulations 1996[64]

7   These Regulations complement the Carriage of Dangerous Goods (Classification, Packaging and Labelling) and Use of Transportable Pressure Receptacles Regulations 1996.[4] Their provisions include requirements for:

(a)   the construction of vehicles;

(b)   information to be received by operators and to be given to drivers;

(c)   the marking of vehicles; and

(d)   the loading, stowage and unloading of consignments.

8   Dangerous substances are those materials:

(a)   included in the *Approved carriage list*[61] produced in association with the 1996 Carriage Regulations mentioned here; or

(b)   with the characteristic properties defined in Schedule 1 of the Carriage of Dangerous Goods (Classification, Packaging and Labelling) and Use of Transportable Pressure Receptacles Regulations 1996.[4]

Chemicals (Hazard Information and Packaging for Supply) Regulations 1994[5] (as amended)

9   These Regulations, commonly referred to as the CHIP Regulations, contain requirements for the supply of chemicals. The Regulations require suppliers of chemicals to:

(a)   classify them, that is, identify their hazards;

(b)   give information about the hazards to the people they supply, both in the form of labels and material safety data sheets; and

(c)   package the chemicals safely.

10   Classifying chemicals according to the CHIP Regulations requires knowledge of physical and chemical properties, and of the health and environmental effects.

11   They are supported by:

(a)   an *Approved supply list*[65] containing agreed classifications for common substances;

(b)   an approved classification and labelling guide;[66]

(c)   an Approved Code of Practice on material safety data sheets;[67]

(d)   and by the guidance publication *CHIP 2 for everyone.*[68]

Control of Pesticides Regulations 1986[11] (as amended)

12   These Regulations, made under the Food and Environment Protection Act 1985,[10] require pesticides to be approved before they may be sold, supplied, used, advertised or stored. In addition sites, storing more than 200 kg, 200 litres or a similar mixed quantity of a pesticide approved for agricultural use, must be under the control of a person holding a recognised certificate of competence.

Control of Industrial Major Accident Hazards Regulations 1984[23] (as amended)

13   These Regulations apply at two levels to certain premises where specified quantities of particular substances are stored or used. The main aim of these Regulations is to prevent major accidents occurring; a secondary objective is to limit the effects of any which do happen. A major accident is a major emission, fire or explosion resulting from uncontrolled developments which leads to serious danger to people or the environment.

14   The general parts of the Regulations apply when more than a specified quantity of a prescribed dangerous substance is stored. In this case, the operator is required to identify major accident hazards, take adequate steps to prevent major accidents and limit the consequences of any which do occur. People working on the site must be provided with any necessary information, training and equipment. Major accidents must be reported to the enforcing authority.

15   If the quantity of a dangerous substance on site exceeds a higher threshold then additional duties apply. A written safety report must be submitted to HSE and an on-site emergency plan prepared. Information must be provided to the local authority for the preparation of an off-site emergency plan and certain information must be provided to the public. The HSE publication HSR21[26] gives guidance on these Regulations.

16   The CIMAH Regulations will be replaced in early 1999 by Regulations implementing a new European Directive, the Seveso II Directive. The new Regulations will have much in common with the CIMAH Regulations.

Control of Substances Hazardous to Health Regulations 1994[16]

17   These Regulations require employers to assess the risks arising from hazardous substances at work and to decide on the measures needed to protect the health of employees. The employer is also required to take appropriate action to prevent or adequately control exposure to the hazardous substance.

18   Substances covered by these Regulations include carcinogenic substances and those which, under the Chemicals (Hazard Information and Packaging for Supply) Regulations,[5] are labelled as very toxic, toxic, harmful, corrosive or irritant. The Regulations also cover dusts, where present in substantial quantities, and those substances assigned occupational exposure limits.

Dangerous Substances (Notification and Marking of Sites) Regulations 1990[57]

19   The purpose of these Regulations is to assist the fire-fighting services by the provision of advance and on-site information on sites containing large quantities of dangerous substances.

20   The Regulations apply to sites containing total quantities of 25 tonnes or more of dangerous substances. They require suitable signs to be erected at access points and at any locations specified by an inspector, and notification to the appropriate fire and enforcing authorities of the presence of any dangerous substance. The HSE publication HSR29[69] gives further guidance.

Electricity at Work Regulations 1989[42]

21   These Regulations impose requirements for electrical systems and equipment, including work activities on or near electrical equipment. They also require electrical equipment which is exposed to any flammable or explosive substance, including flammable liquids or vapours, to be constructed or protected so as to prevent danger.

22   Advice is available in the HSE publication HSR25.[70]

Equipment and Protective Systems Intended for Use in Potentially Explosive Atmospheres Regulations 1996[47]

23   These Regulations are aimed at manufacturers and suppliers. They apply to equipment, protective systems, safety devices, controlling devices, regulating devices and components for use in potentially explosive atmospheres. They require that the equipment is safe, that it meets the essential health and safety requirements, has undergone an appropriate conformity assessment and is affixed with CE marking.

24   There is a lengthy transitional period until 30 June 2003. Manufacturers can, in the meantime, continue to ensure their equipment is safe by other means.

Factories Act 1961[71]

25   The Act defines a 'factory' and contains many general and detailed provisions relating to work activities in factories.

26   Section 31(3) contains specific requirements relating to the opening of plant that contains any explosive, or inflammable gas or vapour under greater than atmospheric pressure. Section 31(4) contains specific requirements relating to the application of heat to plant that has contained any explosive or inflammable substance.

27   'Inflammable' means able to burn with a flame and 'flammable' is generally taken to have the same meaning as 'inflammable'. Inflammable substances and vapours include flammable liquids and their vapours as defined in this guidance book.

Fire Certificates (Special Premises) Regulations 1976[72]

28   These Regulations apply at premises where certain quantities of hazardous materials are processed, used or stored.

29   Where these Regulations apply, they take the place of the Fire Precautions Act 1971[49] and the Fire Precautions (Workplace) Regulations 1997.[41] They designate HSE as the enforcing authority for matters relating to general fire precautions. Further guidance on general fire precautions for premises subject to these Regulations is available from HSE.[73]

Fire Precautions Act 1971[49]

30   This Act controls what have become known as the 'general fire precautions', covering the means of escape in case of fire, the means for ensuring the means of escape can be used safely and effectively, the means for fighting fires, and the means for giving warning in the case of fire, and the training of staff in fire safety. The Act allows the presence of flammable liquids to be taken into account when considering general fire precautions.

31   The Act is enforced by the fire authorities, and further guidance can be found in a Home Office publication.[74]

Fire Precautions (Workplace) Regulations 1997[41]

32   These Regulations require employers to safeguard the safety of employees in case of fire, including the general fire precautions. They require the employer to plan measures to fight fire, and to nominate employees to implement the planned measures, train them and provide them with suitable equipment. They also require contacts to be made with the external emergency services, particularly as regards rescue work and fire fighting.

33   The Regulations are enforced by the fire authorities and apply to all workplaces as defined in the Health and Safety at Work etc Act 1974,[2] unless they are specifically mentioned in the 1997 Regulations as an 'excepted workplace'.

34   Before these Regulations came into force, outdoor storage areas were not necessarily covered by existing fire legislation. In such cases, the requirement for adequate general fire precautions came under the Health and Safety at Work etc Act 1974[2] and were enforced by HSE or the local authorities.

Fire Services Act 1947[56]

35   The purpose of the Act is to ensure the provision of an efficient UK-wide emergency service. It details the requirements for the structure of the service, the duties and powers of fire authorities and measures to secure the availability of an adequate water supply in the event of fire.

Health and Safety at Work etc Act 1974[2]

36   This Act is concerned with the health, safety and welfare of people at work and with protecting those who are not at work (members of the public etc) from risks to their health and safety arising from work activities. The general duties in sections 2 to 4 and 6 to 8 of this Act apply to all work activities which are the subject of this guidance book.

37   The Act is enforced either by the HSE or by local authorities as determined by the Health and Safety (Enforcing Authority) Regulations 1989.[75] Storage operations are enforced by local authorities unless the main business is the storage of dangerous goods, in which case HSE is the enforcing authority.

Health and Safety (Safety Signs and Signals) Regulations 1996[50]

38   These Regulations bring into force the EC Safety Signs Directive (92/58/EEC) on the provision and use of safety signs at work. They cover various means of communicating health and safety information. They require employers to provide specific safety signs whenever there is a risk that has not been avoided or controlled by other means, for example by engineering controls and safe systems of work.

39   The Regulations apply to all places and activities where people are employed. However, they exclude signs and labels used in connection with the supply of substances, products and equipment or the transport of dangerous goods. Guidance on these Regulations is available in an HSE publication.[76]

Highly Flammable Liquids and Liquefied Petroleum Gases Regulations 1972[6]

40   These Regulations apply when liquids, which have a flashpoint of less than 32°C and which support combustion (when tested in the prescribed manner), are present at premises subject to the Factories Act 1961.[71] The Regulations contain provisions for:

(a)   precautions to be taken during storage;

(b)   precautions to be taken against spills and leaks;

(c)   controls for sources of ignition in areas where accumulations of vapours may occur;

(d)   means to prevent the escape of vapours;

(e)   dispersal of dangerous concentrations of vapours;

(f)   controls on smoking.

Management of Health and Safety at Work Regulations 1992[1]

41   These Regulations require employers and the self-employed to assess the risks to employees and others who may be affected by their undertakings, so that they can decide what measures need to be taken to comply with health and safety law.

42   The Regulations go on to require you to implement appropriate arrangements for managing health and safety. Health surveillance (where appropriate), emergency planning, and the provision of information and training are also required. An Approved Code of Practice[27] gives guidance on these Regulations.

Notification of Installations Handling Hazardous Substances Regulations 1982 (NIHHS)[77]

43   These Regulations require premises with specified quantities of particular substances to be notified to HSE. Following the Planning (Hazardous Substances) Act 1990[78] and Regulations 1992,[79] the presence of NIHHS Schedule 1 substances and quantities, together with some from CIMAH Schedule 3,[23] on, over or under land requires consent from hazardous substances authorities.

44   Similar provisions apply in Scotland.

Planning (Hazardous Substances) Act 1990[78] and Regulations 1992[79]

45   These Regulations specify that a hazardous substances consent is required from the appropriate hazardous substances authority for the presence on, over or under land of specified amounts of hazardous substances. Similar provisions apply in Scotland.

Plant Protection Products Regulations 1995[12] (as amended)

46   These Regulations implement the requirements of the Plant Protection Products Directive 91/414/EEC. This is for a community wide authorisation system, whereby plant protection products may not be placed on the market or used unless authorised by a member state under the Directive.

Plant Protection Products (Basic Conditions) Regulations 1997[13]

47   Approval for storage and advertisement of plant protection products is given under these Regulations. They ensure that equivalent controls to those under the Control of Pesticides Regulations 1986[11] are in place for plant protection products. This includes the requirement for sites, storing more than 200 kg, 200 litres or a similar mixed quantity of a plant protection product approved for agricultural use, to be under the control of a person holding a recognised certificate of competence.

Provision and Use of Work Equipment Regulations 1992[80] (to be replaced by the Provision and Use of Work Equipment Regulations 1998)

48   These Regulations aim to ensure the provision of safe work equipment and its safe use. They include general duties covering the selection of suitable equipment, maintenance, information, instructions and training. They also address the need for equipment to control selected hazards. They require employers to ensure that people using work equipment are not exposed to hazards arising from its use.

REFERENCES AND FURTHER READING

References

1   *Management of Health and Safety at Work Regulations 1992* SI 1992/2051 HMSO 1992 ISBN 0 11 025051 6

2   *Health and Safety at Work etc Act 1974 Ch 37* HMSO 1974 ISBN 0 10 543774 3

3   *5 steps to risk assessment* INDG163 HSE Books 1994 ISBN 0 7176 0904 9

4   *Carriage of Dangerous Goods (Classification, Packaging and Labelling) and Use of Transportable Pressure Receptacles Regulations 1996* SI 1996/2092 HMSO 1996 ISBN 0 11 062923 X

5   *The Chemicals (Hazard Information and Packaging for Supply) Regulations 1994* SI 1994/3247 HMSO 1994 ISBN 0 11 043877 9 as amended by *The Chemicals (Hazard Information and Packaging for Supply) (Amendment) Regulations 1996* SI 1996/1092 HMSO 1996 ISBN 0 11 054570 2 and *The Chemicals (Hazard Information and Packaging for Supply) (Amendment) Regulations 1997* SI 1997/1460 HMSO 1997 ISBN 0 11 063750 X

6   *The Highly Flammable Liquids and Liquefied Petroleum Gases Regulations 1972* SI 1972/917 HMSO 1972 ISBN 0 11 020917 6

7   *Environmental Protection Act 1990* HMSO 1990 ISBN 0 10 544390 5

8   *Water Resources Act 1991 Ch 57* HMSO 1991 ISBN 0 10 545791 4

9   *Control of Pollution Act 1974 Ch 40* HMSO 1974 ISBN 0 10 544074 4

10   *Food and Environment Protection Act 1985 Ch 48* HMSO 1985 ISBN 0 10 544885 0 Part 3

11   *The Control of Pesticides Regulations 1986* SI 1986/1510 HMSO 1986
ISBN 0 11 067510 X as amended by *The Control of Pesticides (Amendment) Regulations 1997*
SI 1997/188 HMSO 1997 ISBN 0 11 063695 3

12   *The Plant Protection Products Regulations 1995* SI 1995/887 HMSO 1995
ISBN 0 11 052865 4

13   *The Plant Protection Products (Basic Conditions) Regulations 1997* SI 1997/189 HMSO
1997 ISBN 0 11 063694 5

14   *Code of Practice for suppliers of pesticides to agriculture, horticulture and forestry*
Ministry of Agriculture, Fisheries and Food 1997 (The Yellow Code)

15   *Guidance on storing pesticides for farmers and other professional users* AIS16
HSE Books 1996

16   *The Control of Substances Hazardous to Health Regulations 1994* SI 1994/3246 HMSO
1994 ISBN 0 11 043721 7

17   United Nations. Economic Commission for Europe. Inland Transport Committee
*European agreement concerning the international carriage of dangerous goods by road
(ADR) and protocol of signature : Volume 1 and 2* ECE/TRANS/115 Stationery Office 1997
ISBN 0 11 941518 6

18   *A guide to the Packaging of Explosives for Carriage Regulations 1991. Guidance on
Regulations* L13 HSE Books 1991 ISBN 0 11 885728 2

19   *The Ionising Radiations Regulations 1985* SI 1985/1333 HMSO 1985
ISBN 0 11 057333 1

20   *Cylinder identification. Part 3: Colour coding system for gas cylinders for use in Europe*
BS EN 1089-3 1997

21   *Storing and handling ammonium nitrate* INDG230 HSE Books 1996

22   *Storage and handling of organic peroxides* CS21 HSE Books 1998 ISBN 0 7176 2403 X

23   *The Control of Industrial Major Accident Hazards Regulations 1984* SI 1984/1902
HMSO 1984 ISBN 0 11 047902 5

24   *General COSHH ACOP (Control of Substances Hazardous to Health), and Carcinogens
ACOP (Control of Carcinogenic Substances) and Biological Agents ACOP (Control of
Biological Agents). Control of Substances Hazardous to Health Regulations 1994. Approved
Codes of Practice* L5 HSE Books 1997 ISBN 0 7176 1308 9

25   *Safety of electrical motor-operated industrial cleaning appliances Part 2: Particular requirements Supplement No 1: Type H industrial vacuum cleaners for dusts hazardous to health* BS 5415 Part 2 Supplement 1: 1986

26   *A guide to the Control of Industrial Major Accident Hazards Regulations 1984* HSR21 HSE Books 1990 ISBN 0 11 885579 4

27   *Management of health and safety at work. The Management of Health and Safety at Work Regulations 1992. Approved Code of Practice* L21 HSE Books 1992 ISBN 0 7176 0412 8

28   *Managing contractors: a guide for employers* HSE Books 1997 ISBN 0 7176 1196 5

29   HSC Oil Industry Advisory Committee *Guidance on permit-to-work systems in the petroleum industry* 3rd edition HSE Books 1997 ISBN 0 7176 1281 3

30   *Permit-to-work systems* INDG98 HSE Books 1997 ISBN 0 7176 1331 3

31   *Guidance for the storage of transportable gas cylinders for industrial use* GN 2 British Compressed Gases Association 1997

32   *The Building Regulations 1991* SI 1991/2768 HMSO 1991 ISBN 0 11 015887 3

33   *The Building Standards (Scotland) Regulations 1990* SI 1990/2179 HMSO 1990 ISBN 0 11 005179 3

34   *Assessment of fire hazards from solid materials and the precautions required for their safe storage and use* HSG64 HSE Books 1991 ISBN 0 11 885654 5

35   *The storage of flammable liquids in containers* HSG51 HSE Books 1998 ISBN 0 7176 1471 9

36   *The keeping of LPG in cylinders and similar containers* CS4 HSE Books 1986 ISBN 0 11 83539 4

37   *Energetic and spontaneously combustible substances - identification and safe handling* HSG131 HSE Books 1995 ISBN 0 7176 0893 X

38   *Safe use and storage of cellular plastics* HSG92 HSE Books 1996 ISBN 0 7176 1115 9

39   *Storage and handling of industrial nitrocellulose* HSG135 HSE Books 1995 ISBN 0 7176 0694 5

40   *The Buildings Regulations 1991. Fire Safety: Approved Document B* HMSO 1991 ISBN 0 11 752313 5

41   *The Fire Precautions (Workplace) Regulations 1997* SI 1997/1840 HMSO 1997 ISBN 0 11 064738 6

42   *The Electricity at Work Regulations 1989* SI 1989/635 HMSO ISBN 0 11 096635 X

43   *Electrical apparatus for explosive gas atmospheres. Part 10: Classification of hazardous areas* BS EN 60079-10: 1996

44   Institute of Petroleum *Area classification code for petroleum installations: model code of safe practice in the petroleum industry part 15* Wiley 1990 ISBN 0 47 192160 2

45   *Electrical apparatus for explosive gas atmospheres. Part 14: Electrical installations in hazardous areas (other than mines)* BS EN 60079-14: 1997

46   *Electricity and flammable substances: A short guide for small businesses* Institution of Chemical Engineers 1989 ISBN 0 85 295250 3

47   *The Equipment and Protective Systems Intended for Use in Potentially Explosive Atmospheres Regulations 1996* SI 1996/192 HMSO 1996 ISBN 0 11 053999 0

48   *Lift trucks in potentially flammable atmospheres* HSG113 HSE Books 1996 ISBN 0 7176 0706 2

49   *Fire Precautions Act 1971 Ch 40* HMSO 1971 ISBN 0 10 544071 X

50   *The Health and Safety (Safety Signs and Signals) Regulations 1996* SI 1996/341 HMSO 1996 ISBN 0 11 054093 X

51   *Fire safety signs, notices and graphic symbols. Part 1: Fire safety signs* BS 5499: Part 1 1990

52   *Portable fire extinguishers* BS EN 3 (6 parts)

53   *Fire detection and alarm systems for buildings* BS 5839 (6 parts)

54   *Fire extinguishing installations and equipment on premises. Part 2: Specification for sprinkler systems* BS 5306: Part 2 1990

55   Smoke Ventilation Association *Guidance for the design of smoke ventilation systems for single storey industrial buildings, including those with mezzanine floors, and high racked storage warehouses* HEVAC Manufacturers Association 1994 ISBN 1 870623 03 7

56   *Fire Services Act 1947 Ch 41* HMSO 1947 ISBN 0 10 850109 4

57   *Dangerous Substances (Notification and Marking of Sites) Regulations 1990* SI 1990/304 HMSO 1990 ISBN 0 11 003304 3

58   *The control of fire-water run-off from CIMAH sites to prevent environmental damage* EH70 HSE Books 1995 ISBN 0 7176 0990 1

59   *Design of containment systems for the prevention of water pollution from industrial incidents* CIRIA Report/IP/21 Construction Industry Research and Information Association 1996

60   *The Control of Industrial Major Accident Hazards Regulations 1984 (CIMAH): Further guidance on emergency plans* HSG25 HSE Books 1985 ISBN 0 11 883831 8

61   *Approved carriage list: information approved for the carriage of dangerous goods by road and rail other than explosives and radioactive material* L90 HSE Books 1996 ISBN 0 7176 1223 6

62   *Approved requirements and test methods for the classification and packaging of dangerous goods for carriage* L88 HSE Books 1996 ISBN 0 7176 1221 X

63   *The Carriage of Dangerous Goods by Road Regulations 1996* SI 1996/2095 HMSO 1996 ISBN 0 11 062926 4

64   *The Carriage of Dangerous Goods by Rail Regulations 1996* SI 1996/2089 HMSO 1996 ISBN 0 11 062919 1

65   *Approved supply list. Information approved for the classification and labelling of substances and preparations dangerous for supply. CHIP 96* L76 HSE Books 1996 ISBN 0 7176 1116 7

66   *Approved guide to the classification and labelling of substances and preparations dangerous for supply - CHIP97* L100 HSE Books 1997 ISBN 0 7176 1366 6

67   *Safety datasheets for substances and preparations dangerous for supply. Guidance on Regulation 6 of the CHIP Regulations 1994. Approved Code of Practice* L62 HSE Books 1990 ISBN 0 7176 0859 X

68   *CHIP 2 for everyone* HSG126 HSE Books 1995 ISBN 0 7176 0857 3

69   *Notification and marking of sites. The Dangerous Substances (Notification and Marking of Sites) Regulations 1990* HSR29 HSE Books 1990 ISBN 0 11 885435 6

70   *Memorandum of guidance on the Electricity at Work Regulations 1989* HSR25 HSE Books 1989 ISBN 0 11 883963 2

71   *Factories Act 1961 Ch 34* HMSO 1961 ISBN 0 10 850027 6

72   *Fire Certificates (Special Premises) Regulations 1976* SI 1976/2003 HMSO 1976 ISBN 0 11 062003 8

73   *Guidance on general fire precautions at premises subject to the Fire Certificates (Special Premises) Regulations 1976* HSE, Gas and Chemical Process Safety Unit 1985 ISBN 0 7176 0249 4

74   *Fire Precautions Act 1971. Guide to fire precautions in existing places of work that require a fire certificate. Factories, offices, shops and railway premises* HMSO 1993 ISBN 0 11 341079 4

75   *The Health and Safety (Enforcing Authority) Regulations 1989* SI 1989/1903 HMSO 1989 ISBN 0 11 097903 6

76   *Safety signs and signals. The Health and Safety (Safety Signs and Signals) Regulations 1996. Guidance on Regulations* L64 HSE Books 1996 ISBN 0 7176 0870 0

77   *The Notification of Installations Handling Hazardous Substances Regulations 1982* SI 1982/1357 HMSO 1982 ISBN 0 11 027357 5

78   *Planning (Hazardous Substances) Act 1990* HMSO 1990 ISBN 0 10 541090 X

79   *Planning (Hazardous Substances) Regulations 1992* SI 1992/656 HMSO 1992 ISBN 0 11 023656 4

80   *The Provision and Use of Work Equipment Regulations 1992* SI 1992/2932 HMSO 1992 ISBN 0 11 025849 5 (to be replaced by the Provision and Use of Work Equipment Regulations 1998)

Further reading

Safe storage, handling and use of special gases in the microelectronics industry CoP 18 British Compressed Gases Association 1988

Guide to good practice for the storage of aerosols in manufacturing/wholesale warehouses and retail stores British Aerosol Manufacturers Association 1989

Guide to warehouse operators - when a CIMAH safety report is required British Chemical Distributors and Traders Association

Safety in action warehousing of chemicals guide British Chemical Distributors and Traders Association 1989

Code of practice for accommodation of building services in ducts BS 8313: 1997

Code of practice for fire precautions in the chemical and allied industries BS 5908: 1990

Safety signs and colours BS 5378 (in three parts)

A guide to safe warehousing for the European chemical industry European Council of Chemical Manufacturers' Federation 1987

Guidelines for safe warehousing of substances with hazardous characteristics Chemical Industries Association 1983

Compendium of fire safety data. No 2: Industrial and process fire safety Fire Protection Association

Guidelines for safe warehousing of pesticides International Group of National Associations of Manufacturers of Agrochemical Products (GIFAP) 1988

Radioactive Substances Act 1960. A guide to the administration of the Act HMSO 1982 ISBN 0 11 751625 2

Chlorine from drums and cylinders HSG40 HSE Books 1987 ISBN 0 11 883968 3 (under revision)

Formula for health and safety: Guidance for small and medium-sized firms in the chemical industry HSG166 HSE Books 1997 ISBN 0 7176 0996 0

Health and safety in retail and wholesale warehouses HSG76 HSE Books 1992 ISBN 0 11 885731 2

Occupational exposure limits EH40/98 HSE Books 1998 ISBN 0 7176 1474 3

Prepared for...emergency INDG246 HSE Books 1997 ISBN 0 7176 1330 5

Safe handling of combustible dusts HSG103 HSE Books 1994 ISBN 0 7176 0725 9

The fire at Allied Colloids Limited. A report of HSE's investigation into the fire at Allied Colloids Ltd, Low Moor, Bradford on 21 July 1992 HSE Books 1993 ISBN 0 7176 0707 0

The protection of persons against ionising radiation arising from any work activity. The Ionising Radiation Regulations 1985. Approved Code of Practice L58 HSE Books 1985 ISBN 0 7176 0508 6

The safe use and handling of flammable liquids HSG140 HSE Books 1996
ISBN 0 7176 0967 7

The storage of flammable liquids in tanks HSG176 HSE Books 1998
ISBN 0 7176 1470 0

IChemE 'The protection of warehouses against fires' *Loss Prevention Bulletin* December 1988
(084)

IChemE 'The Sandoz warehouse fire' *Loss Prevention Bulletin* (075)

Loss Prevention Council *Fire and hazardous substances* Library of fire safety volume 2 Fire
Protection Association 1994 ISBN 0 902167 61 8

Loss Prevention Council *Guide to fire safety signs* Library of fire safety volume 4 Fire
Protection Association 1996 ISBN 0 902167 87 1

Recommendations for hot work RC7 Loss Prevention Council 1994

Recommendations for fire safety in the storage and use of flammable liquids
Part 1 General principles RC20A
Part 2 Storage of flammable liquids in drums, cans and other containers RC20B
Loss Prevention Council 1997

Preece Consulting Group 'The forgotten hazards: services in warehouses' *Loss Prevention
Bulletin* December 1988 (084)

Waeckerlig H 'The aftermath of the Sandoz fire' *Fire Prevention Journal* May 1987 (199)

Ward R 'A survey of major fires in warehouses containing dangerous chemicals'
Fire Prevention Journal December 1984 (175)

The future availability and accuracy of the references listed in this publication cannot be
guaranteed.

GLOSSARY

Combustible: Capable of burning in air when ignited.

Corrosive: Capable of destroying human tissue or causing normal construction materials to corrode at an excessive rate.

Enforcing authority: The authority with responsibility for enforcing the Health and Safety at Work etc Act 1974[2] and other relevant statutory provisions.

Flammable: Capable of burning with a flame.

Flammable range: The concentration of a flammable vapour in air falling between the upper and lower explosion limits.

Flashpoint: The minimum temperature at which a liquid, under specific test conditions, gives off sufficient flammable vapour to ignite momentarily on the application of an ignition source.

Hazard: The disposition of a thing, a condition or a situation to cause injury. The 'injury' of concern is physical injury and/or ill-health to people, though this may be accompanied by harm to property and the environment.

Hazardous area: An area where flammable or explosive gas or vapour-air mixtures (often referred to as explosive gas-air mixtures) are, or may be expected to be, present in quantities which require special precautions to be taken against the risk of ignition.

Incendive: Having sufficient energy to ignite a flammable mixture.

Interceptor (also known as separator): A device installed in a surface water drainage system to separate out any immiscible solvents, and thus prevent them from reaching public drains, sewers or water courses.

Lower explosion limit (LEL): The minimum concentration of vapour in air below which propagation of a flame will not occur in the presence of an ignition source. Also referred to as the lower flammable limit or lower explosive limit.

Occupational exposure limit (OEL): The limits of concentration in the air of substances hazardous to health, averaged over a specified time period.

Reasonably practicable: The degree of risk in a particular job or workplace needs to be balanced against the time, trouble, cost and physical difficulty of taking measures to avoid or reduce the risk. Measures must be taken to eliminate or control the risks unless it is clear that the cost of doing so is grossly disproportionate to the level of risk. However, the ability to pay for additional control measures is not a deciding factor as to whether they are necessary.

Risk: The chance of something adverse happening where 'something' refers to a particular consequence of the manifestation of a hazard.

Risk assessment: The process of identifying the hazards present in any undertaking (whether arising from work activities or other factors) and those people likely to be affected by them, and of evaluating the extent of the risks involved, bearing in mind whatever precautions are already being taken.

Toxic: Poisonous.

Upper explosion limit (UEL): The maximum concentration of vapour in air above which the propagation of a flame will not occur. Also referred to as the upper flammable limit or upper explosive limit.

Vapour: The gaseous phase released by evaporation from a material that is a liquid at normal temperatures and pressure.

Zone: The classified part of a hazardous area, representing the probability of a flammable vapour (or gas) and air mixture being present.

Printed and published by the Health and Safety Executive   1/04   C10